DESPERATE HOUSEWIVES
of the Bible

O.T. Edition

Robert Strand

Desperate Housewives of the Bible, O.T. Edition
by Robert J. Strand
Copyright ©2006 Robert J. Strand

ISBN 1-58169-189-0
For Worldwide Distribution
Printed in the U.S.A.

Evergreen Press
P.O. Box 191540 • Mobile, AL 36619

TABLE OF CONTENTS

DEDICATION

To all the wonderful housewives in my family who have
lived out life's lessons in the finest sense of the word. They
are wonderful models for others, and many lives have been
touched by their example. And so to my wife Donna,
daughter Cheriee, grandmother Gina, mother Ruth,
aunts Doris, Evangeline, Julie, Edith and Ruth,
daughters-in-law Becky and Jennifer, and
sisters-in-law Judy and Debbie.

Also to housewives everywhere and to their spouses
who have been curious enough to want to know about how
others have handled desperate situations.

INTRODUCTION

Women through the ages have agonized over many of the same issues: child birthing, worrying about kids, longing for affection, needing a life's partner, searching for answers, infertility, jealousy, anger, disappointments, and circumstances beyond their control. Some of these women have created their desperate situations; others have been completely innocent victims of events over which they have not been able to exercise control.

We will be taking a look at many women from the Old Testament and their stories, stories that reveal so much that is helpful. These women have not been selected because they were perfect. Not really! These women make for an interesting cast of characters and contrasts—some are prominent, while some are obscure and largely unknown. These women portray for us interesting slices of life—some were prostitutes, others ruthless queens, prophetesses, wealthy women, leaders, poor women, widowed women, mothers, aunts, grandmothers, young women, old women and even abused women. But all are significant and have a story needing to be told as well as classic wisdom from ages past to apply to our lives in the 21st century.

The style in which we'll be looking at these women could best be described as *midrashim*. What does this mean? *Midrash* comes from a Hebrew word literally meaning "to go in search of" or "to inquire about." Midrashim came about as a result of Jewish rabbis going in search of the real meaning of scripture. It was a way in which the gaps were filled in. Much of this style of storytelling, teaching or preaching came from the sermons given in their synagogues. There are many gaps in the typical biblical story because it seems as though the Jewish scribes were men of few words. Remember, they wrote by hand without help from computers or other technologies. It was a laborious labor of love. Biblical stories, with their panoramic sweep of thousands of years, mainly give us the facts and their essence without much detail or background. To illustrate, Solomon who was the wisest human ever to walk on this earth, according to rabbis, supposedly knew some three thousand stories for every verse of Scripture and about a thousand and five interpretations for each story. When the "canon" of the Bible's New Testament was completed, there were four different stories about Jesus contained in Matthew, Mark, Luke and John. And we are enriched by having these four looks at the ministry and His life.

The Bible provides a fascinating look at people and how they have related to this world and to their God. We know the stories of prominent men in the Bible and the roles they have played, but too many of us have long overlooked the role of women and how they fit into the plan of God. We shall make some interesting discoveries about women and their relationship to God as well as others, and about God's love for them. Perhaps in looking at their responses we can take another look at our response to God.

The title of this book is borrowed from one of the most popular television sit-coms to come down the tube in a long time, "Desperate Housewives." This title may have caught your attention, but it goes beyond just being an attention getter. My attempt is to bring you into a different arena—an arena where desperation is overcome by eternal answers.

Robert J. Strand
Springfield, Missouri USA

CHAPTER ONE

EVE

Desperate for a taste of forbidden fruit

What must it have been like to be the very first woman to set foot on this earth and the first housewife to take care of a family? We can only imagine.

There is not a figure in history who has been blamed more than Eve. Many have said if it were not for her falling for the serpent's line, we'd still be in the Garden. I'm not so sure about that.

Scripture: *Genesis 1:26-31; 2:4-25; 3:1-6; 4:1-26; I Timothy 2:13-14*

HER SIDE OF THE STORY...

I came into this world fully formed and completely mature, except for one thing—Adam and I were not born; we were created and so we have no history, making us quite unique. God had created Adam first and said it was very good. But I think that when God was planning a mate for Adam, He thought to himself, "That was good, but I think I can do just a little bit better." So here I am—the second edition, softer, more rounded, more beautiful. When I was presented to Adam, you

1

should have seen the look on his face! It really was love at first sight.

You might be interested in our home. It was the most gorgeous piece of real estate in the entire world. We had every kind of tree and fruit you can possibly imagine. The landscaping was unbelievable. It truly, in every sense of the word, was a garden put together by God. The temperature was exactly right for us, and the animals were something else—friendly and ever so much fun. Adam named them, and I must say he did a great job. Some of them must have taken real thought and imagination, but he was up to the challenge. Who else could have come up with names like giraffe, hippo, elephant, macaw, platypus, lion, monkey and have them seem to fit so exactly?

What a wonderful world! And we had it all to ourselves. We picked and ate juicy fruit, crunchy nuts, and delicious veggies, and drank from the crystal clear springs (no, your Starbucks hadn't been invented yet). What a life! Oh, we were busy tending the garden, but living was just great. God visited with us often—what more could we ask for?

There was only one "no-no." It was just a tree, but, oh, did it have wonderful, enticing fruit! God said it was the "tree of knowledge of good and evil." What's evil? What's good? I really didn't have a clue back then. God warned us that if we ate from this tree we would die. I had no idea what He meant.

The snake said we would not die, but we would become like God! Now that is some kind of thought—to be powerful like God and be able to create and control creation.

I'm getting ahead of myself. As I said, we had access to everything except this tree in the middle of the garden. This was the first forbidden thing I was ever presented with. "You must not eat from the tree...." That was like telling kids they can't have a cookie until they finish their supper. Maybe God created us in this way—whatever we are told not to do, we want to do. If this tree was so bad for us, why did it appear so beautiful and desirable?

Anyhow, Adam and I had a great life enjoying each other's company, along with the companionship of the animals and birds. There was no fear, and everyone and everything worked together in harmony. But, as you probably guessed, this didn't last too long.

It happened on a day like any other day. Adam was on an errand to another part of the garden and I was alone. I strolled to the middle of the garden and in front of me was the special tree! I was just getting a better look at it, but all the while keeping my distance. Then the snake appeared. I guess you probably hate snakes, but believe me, back then the snake was beautiful and more crafty than any other of God's created animals, and that is really saying something. This snake was something else; it talked with me. I was intrigued for it was one fascinating conversation.

When the snake said, "God didn't really tell you not to eat from this tree, now did He?" I began to think.

I replied, "God said we could eat from all the trees except this one, and if we touched it we would die." (Remember, I still didn't know what "die" meant; it really sounded mysterious.)

"You won't die," he assured me, "but God has been holding something back from you. He knows when you eat this fruit you will be like Him because then you will know all about good and evil."

Now you might think this conversation all happened in a matter of a few moments, but it continued on and off for a number of days. Each time I met with the snake under the tree, the fruit looked more inviting and more intriguing.

Then the day came when I timidly reached for a piece of fruit, just one piece, and grasped it in my hands. Nothing happened, but, oh, did it ever look appealing! I held it a long time, turning it round and round, and smelled its beautiful fragrance. The texture was so smooth; it was like nothing I had ever touched. I cautiously brought it to my mouth and took a bite. It had a snap and crunch to it, and wonderful juice ran down my hand and arm—it was delicious beyond anything I had ever eaten. I kept on eating until it was all gone! I took another piece and another and another until I was full. Still I was okay, and nothing like dying had happened to me—yet.

I grabbed a handful of the fruit and ran to Adam. I convinced him it was all right to eat it since I had already done so and nothing had happened to me. When I pushed it on him, he looked like he wanted to please me and ate of this unbelievable fruit. What a picnic we had that day!

Then it slowly began to happen—we looked at each other and at ourselves and realized, "WE WERE NAKED!" Up until this point we had no shame, only innocence, but now we knew we were naked. Something had to be done!

About this time, we knew we had to hide from God who was taking his regular walk in the garden. We heard His voice calling us, "Where are you?" But how can you hide from God?

What had we done? What had I done? To cover our nakedness, God invented clothes, although, to tell you the truth, the fig leaves he used itched horribly.

We all paid the consequences for what we had done. The snake was cursed and had to crawl in the dust on his belly all the way down to your day. To me, God said, "You will have pains in bearing children, and you will desire a husband." To my dear husband who had listened to me, God said, "The ground is cursed, and you will survive by the sweat of your brow all your days, and all humanity will have to do the same." (There were no government hand-outs back then.)

I went from being Eve, "the mother of life" in the Garden

of Eden, located in Paradise, to being Mrs. Adam, some place east of the Flaming Sword Gate, somewhere in Southwest Asia. It was "Paradise Enjoyed" turned into "Paradise Lost, Forever."

And am I ever sorry! I sure messed up my life as well as yours, too. We tried the blame game with God, but it didn't work. Adam said it was me, I said it was the snake, and the snake has been passing the blame ever since to any and all who might listen.

After our fiasco in the garden, life with all its pains and sorrows began. We were unceremoniously moved out of there by the angels. In our new land Adam worked from sunup to sundown and sure did sweat a lot. You should have seen the laundry, and me without a top loading machine! I began having babies with lots of pain and no hospital birthing centers with their painkillers in sight.

My first two children were certainly a disappointment. Speaking about firsts, my son committed the first murder, and I'm sure you know that the victim was his brother. I thought our sorrow at being thrown out of the garden was bad, but it was nothing compared to the agony of this family feud. I was ready to make another start at life and living. Fortunately God heard my prayer.

Seth was born, and he brought new hope and helped take away the sorrow—he really was a new start for our family! He was followed by a whole new generation of people who began to try to live like God had wanted us to do all along.

Yes, my family is like the rest of the human family that followed us—with both good and bad times. And I certainly missed the enjoyment of the garden all the days of my life. I really made a mess of God's blueprint for the human race. Sorry. But you know what, although I may have been the first, I was not the last to trash my life. I will be forever grateful that God gave me a new start.

WISDOM FROM EVE FOR 21st CENTURY LIVING:

It's not a matter of *if* we will mess up but rather, it's *when* we mess up, there is hope and help for us! Yes, Eve had a new start, and we, too, can experience a new start. It's a matter of facing up to our failures and asking a God who loves us to help us with a new start. It's a matter of getting up one more time than we have fallen. We may have flunked a test, but the final exam hasn't been given yet!

Eve's family crisis, with God's help, in turn, led to a new beginning. Like so many sorrowing mothers of this world, when she was faced with tragedy, she learned to turn to God for comfort, help and answers. Her grief over losing her most promising son, Abel, and the lost hope of her wayward son, Cain, must have caused her pain beyond belief. Yet she learned that God is not only just, but He is also the God of second chances.

CHAPTER TWO

ABIGAIL

Desperate to save her household

 Not every marriage works; sometimes a real mis-match is consummated. The marriage of Abigail and Nabal is an example. Why did she marry this turkey? In her days, often the bride to be had no choice. Nabal may have been considered a real catch by her parents because he was a rich man and used to getting what he wanted.

In this man is embodied all the attributes that are repulsive in the male species. He was an arrogant hot-head, nasty tongued, a selfish drunkard, and a fool—I mean, a real fool. Abigail, on the other hand, was a woman of refinement, grace, intelligence, resourcefulness and beauty. She was a woman with a most appealing character and faith.

Scripture: *I Samuel 25:2-42; Psalm 30:10-12*

HER SIDE OF THE STORY...

Well, just where do I begin? While I was growing up, my home was nothing special; it was much like others in Israel. I had good parents who taught me well, especially my mother, who taught me a whole lot about getting along with men.

One more thing, it helps to be beautiful as well as charming. Beauty helped me get along quite well in life. Oh, yes, my dad doted on me as his very special daughter. He made sure I had what I needed to hone my skills—charm school, finishing school, cooking school and an opportunity to study the Torah. I had a wonderful childhood.

But all of that began to change in my teen years. Because of my supposed beauty, so I was told, suitors began hanging around our place. These guys were so much fun to watch as they appealed to my father. I would listen through the tent or hide behind the barn to hear what they had to say. It was a hoot! But Daddy turned them all down—none of them had a dowry worthy of his beautiful daughter. I don't know just how it happened that the richest codger in the area came calling. But he did and it changed my life. He was used to getting what he wanted, and he wanted me for a wife. So he made a deal with my father and offered a dowry that Daddy, in his right mind, just could not refuse. In fact, it really set up my dad for retirement in his old age.

He told me, "Abigail, honey, this guy may be a real turkey, but he is the richest turkey in the world, and he's made an offer I can't turn down. I'm sorry. Yes, I know he's a lot older than you are, but I hope you'll be happy."

What could I do—I had no choice. So we got married, and it was a huge spectacle. Talk about a show of wealth! I was supposed to be the center of all this fuss. Finally came our marriage night—to say the least it was a disappointment, and I'll not bore you with details. And we were supposed to live happily ever after. It quickly proved to be "unhappily ever after."

How can a woman live with a man who is described as being surly and mean in all his dealings with people? Not only that, he fancied himself to be like a king. He was so arrogant no one could talk sense into him. He was a fool of the fools;

yes, a rich fool, but still a fool. If he had not inherited his wealth, he wouldn't have had any. He had a mean mouth, always shooting it off and getting himself in trouble; but because of his money, he got away with it, that is, until he tangled with David!

What a day to change my whole life! One of our trusted servants came running to me to tell me the events that had just taken place. Nabal had turned down the normal request of David's men to share in the abundance of harvest. It was a matter of hospitality in our day. Not only did Nabal turn down this reasonable request, but he hurled insults at David and his men.

Men being men, they can't let insults like this go unanswered or unchallenged. Something about how the male psyche is wired, I think. Yes, I'd heard a lot about David and his men and knew there was trouble coming our way. Big trouble! Deadly force kind of trouble! At the least, every male in our employ would probably be killed along with my fool of a husband!

What could I do? I remembered something Mother always said that the way to a man's heart is through his stomach so I quickly whipped up something for David and his men. The females in Israelite homes (some things never change) prepared the meals, so I called my gals together, and we whipped up this little lunch: 200 loaves of bread, two skins of wine, five dressed sheep (not clothes, just killed, cleaned, skinned, and ready to barbecue), five bushels of popped corn, 100 cakes of raisins and 200 cakes of pressed figs.

"Hurry, girls, get this picnic lunch on our donkeys!" And away we went at a fast trot. Good thing I had spent time in cooking school or I couldn't have pulled it off that quickly.

When we came to a mountain ravine, there was David and his men riding hard toward us. I could hear David shouting and spitting out venom of what he would do to Nabal and all our servants—nothing less than killing every male! Wow! Turn on the charm, turn on the smile, turn on the humility, turn on the sweet talk, turn it all on, and, at the same time, turn it on David. You know, he was one good looking guy with his hair flying and fire in his eyes riding his horse down the ravine. It was a matter of survival—life or death. I definitely didn't want to botch this up.

I jumped off my donkey and bowed down as I waited for David. This stopped him as soon as he saw me. I had his attention. Then I took it one step further: I fell at his feet and said, "Blame me and don't pay any attention to my fool of a husband! His name is 'Fool' and he acts like one and folly is his modus operandi. I'm sorry, I didn't see your men nor hear their request...yada, yada, yada." You catch the drift.

I understand that I gave the longest speech the Bible ever recorded by any woman. If I must say so myself, it sure turned out right—it was the exact right thing to say to avert total tragedy for my household. It wasn't long before all the anger had drained from David's face. What a relief!

It was quite a picnic we had that day. David was gracious, and did I already say it—he's a stud and a charmer. Finally it was time to leave, and he sent me and my girls off in peace with the promise that he would not destroy my husband nor our business. Whew...

The story doesn't end here. I got home only to find my husband in high spirits and stone drunk! There was no use talking to him when he was in this condition. Through the years I had found that it was always best to talk to my husband in the morning after he's slept it off. So I went to bed, thinking about David. Did I say that David was gorgeous? Oh, yes.

In the morning, my husband was sober, so I told him

everything! The more I told him, the more he looked like he was about to burst or something. In fact, his heart failed, and we had to carry him to his bed. He was out of it—he couldn't talk or even move, and mercifully in ten days he kicked the bucket. Really, I guess I should have been sad, but for me and the servants, it's like we'd all been set free. We had to be careful not to celebrate too joyfully as we went through the ritual of saying our last good-byes. It was more like sighs of relief than a loving last good-bye, although it really was sad to see a life end like his did.

Life became wonderful! In a few short days, I got a special card from, of all people, David! In it, he proposed marriage! This time it was up to me to decide if I wanted to be married to him or not. It was so sweet and charming and romantic. It took me about a New York minute (now where did that come from?) to decide. If you thought I was in a rush to pack that picnic lunch, you should have seen us get ready to send back our reply.

Of course, we had to take time to prepare—take a quick bath, get the right outfit, put on the best jewelry, fix my hair, put on my make-up just right and use the best perfume. You should have been there—six giddy women all attempting to get me ready at once! What a happy mess! By this time the guys had our donkeys ready and away my servants and I went!

I don't know about this next thing—it might work in your culture, maybe not, but the first thing we did was wash the feet of all of David's entourage. Did they ever love it!

Then David made his appearance. I bowed again but the way he looked at me, my knees turned to rubber. He gathered me into his arms and well, you know the rest of the story. Oh, yes, I wasn't his first wife; I hope this doesn't bother you too much. You see she had been taken from him and given to another guy. She was just a token, trophy wife.

Yes, we really did live happily ever after. I became a queen! When David was crowned king of all of Israel, I shared in the celebration. I hope you could agree, I was a natural queen with intelligence, wisdom, grace and beauty. And we truly did live a blessed life.

WISDOM FROM ABIGAIL FOR 21st CENTURY LIVING:

Abigail may have felt suffocated and stifled when paired with such a surly and mean first husband. These circumstances didn't stop her from becoming a gracious and caring person. Because of her quick thinking and perception, she averted a tragedy which was about to be inflicted on not only her husband, but also her innocent servants. She kept her attitude right in life's tough circumstances. She remained loyal to her God and His principles guided her life.

Keep the faith—you never know when God has something else in mind for your life! Life can be turned upside down in a moment for good or bad!

CHAPTER THREE

ABISHAG

Desperate to win

 Very little is known about this charming and gorgeous lady. Her name means "My father wanders" or perhaps "My father causes wandering." Interesting name for a girl. She was a Shunammitess from the area of Issachar.

Her claim to fame was nothing more than she was beautiful and would make a good practical nurse for an aging king. Apparently this strategy didn't work too well because King David died soon after this cute nurse had taken on her duties.

Scripture: *I Kings 1:1-4, 15; 2:13-25*

HER SIDE OF THE STORY...

Yes, go ahead and say it—I became the world's first human hot water bottle. Well, maybe not the first, but perhaps the most famous human hot water bottle. Hold on...I'm getting a bit ahead of my story.

I was born into a normal family who happened to live in an area called "Shunem," which is located at the southwest foot of Little Mount Hermon about three miles north of Jezreel. It was a beautiful and wealthy area. Not much of historical value happened here. You should know that it was here in a widow's home that the prophet Elisha stayed. That's an interesting story you must read sometime because a boy was raised back to life there. Now that was cool. It was also where the Philistine army made their camp before the last battle in which King Saul fought and lost his life. Enough of history, it can be so boring.

Anyway, I was raised like any good Jewish girl. I learned how to do all the expected things—how to be a good wife, daughter, cook, seamstress and much more. It was a humble beginning, but all that changed with the beauty contest.

It was a sad time for all of us because we knew our wonderful king was dying. He was old, so old he couldn't keep warm even in our warm climate, so old they couldn't find enough covers to keep him warm.

Leave it to a bunch of men to come up with this solution—they put their heads together and decided he needed a young, pretty virgin to keep him company and be his nurse. They thought that if he laid with a young thing it would warm him up. You know, our king always had an eye for beautiful women and married some of them. In fact, I may well have been his twentieth wife! Here I am, getting ahead of myself, again. Anyway, his advisors thought it might work wonders for his health, just like it had in the past.

So they announced this beauty contest for all the young and beautiful virgins of Israel. Sure, the thought crossed my mind that I'd like to be selected as "Miss Israel." But so did every other girl in our country. The dates were announced, the judges chosen and the venue was set. We practiced our posture, fixed our hair, our make-up, and our clothes. It was to be an evening gown contest along with the interview. Our mothers were all in a toot, too. My mother insisted on engaging a designer for the gown. "Nothing but the best for our little princess."

You could have cut the tension with a knife, particularly among the mothers who hovered and cajoled, primped and coached, cried and shouted, and all this was directed for the benefit of the judges. You know all about Jewish mothers, I'm sure. My mother sure made waves. It was sort of embarrassing, but it couldn't have hurt.

I must admit, I was nervous when the grand prize was announced—to become a hot water bottle to the king. There was nothing sexual about this, so to make it legal, the winner would also be married to the king in a quiet ceremony. It was the most fabulous prize ever offered in the Miss Israel contests.

The judges had put us through our paces, and then they gathered around the table. Lots of noise, some shouting, a bit of finger pointing, more writing and tabulating. It seemed to take forever. Finally they were ready to announce the winner.

The fifth runner-up went to my best friend, Adah; the fourth runner-up was awarded to a nobody, Elizabeth; the third runner-up was another unknown girl who was quite cute, Naarah. Tension was building. The second runner-up went to a girl, well, what should I say and still be kind, what did they see in her, Miss Uppity, Sarai; the first runner-up was a complete surprise, Zilpah. Yes, I must say I was disappointed; I had so wanted to be the chosen one.

The judge took his time clearing his throat, shuffling his papers, putting on his reading glasses, and then taking them off and cleaning them. The crowd was poised on the front of each chair. Oh, this was too much. He cleared his throat and looked around and began, "It is with a great pleasure of mine to introduce to you, Miss Israel of 961 B.C. I present to you the lovely, the beautiful, the talented Miss Abishag...MISS ISRAEL OF 961!" Awesome! There was thunderous applause. I was floored! I couldn't believe it! Everybody was jumping and shouting and crying and celebrating all at the same time!

Things happened very quickly, I said good bye to my parents and gathered a few things. They told me I would have a brand new wardrobe, all designer things, and put me in a fast chariot, and I was on my way to Jerusalem! On the way to the palace there were people lining the sidewalks, to get a look at the reigning Miss Israel. It was a whirl—fresh bath, new clothes, new hair-do, perfume, quick run-through on protocol with the king, what I could and could not do as his nurse/human hot water bottle.

I looked at myself in the mirror and had to admit that it was quite a transformation from being little Miss Nothing to becoming Miss Israel and the next wife of the king. When we entered his chamber, he raised himself on one elbow and for a moment or two, there was a flash of the old David. He was excited, alive, and approving of what he saw, at least I'd like to think so. There was a quick ceremony, just to make things legal, by the prophet Nathan, and then I was led to the bed to lay and warm up the king. I really didn't know what to do, but there was an older nurse nearby who was coaching me on how to do my job. It seemed to work for a while. It was fun, but what a different lifestyle it is to live in a palace and be the wife of the king. I was really a queen and the last and youngest of his harem! Oh, yes, some of his old wives were a bit upset at me, the newcomer, warming him up.

Time quickly passed. After awhile I couldn't even warm him up enough and he died. His funeral, to say the least, was some kind of a grand affair beyond anything I had ever witnessed. Oh yes, his last act before he died was to install his son, Solomon, as the new king. (Solomon sure didn't need a human water bottle to keep him warm.)

After the hubbub had died down, another of King David's sons wanted to marry me. His name was Adonijah, and he used the new king's mother to request my hand in marriage. I didn't understand all that happened behind the scenes, but Adonijah was killed over me because Solomon saw through him. It was something called treason. It was considered a crime that Adonijah wanted to marry his father's secondary wife. It might have been okay for me, but I didn't want to be another pawn in the palace intrigue.

There's not much more I can say of my life. I never married, but I sure inherited a whole lot of land and money, and made life easier for my mom and dad. I remained a virgin for the rest of my life and had an easy lifestyle to my dying day.

WISDOM FROM ABISHAG FOR 21st CENTURY LIVING:

Be ready for change that may come your way unexpectedly. You can wake up any ordinary kind of a day, and in a moment everything can and might change.

It happens all the time. Therefore, you need something that is a constant, something you can count on, something to be with you through thick and thin and all the twists and turns of life. What is it? A personal relationship with the King of all kings, the Lord of all lords—Jesus Christ, who is the same yesterday today and forever.

Chapter Four

SARAH

Desperate to bear a child

 Sarah is an interesting study in the highs and lows of life. She laughed and she sorrowed; she showed both anger and submission. Sarah was a life-long beauty. As a child, her beauty shone with flawless skin, bright shiny clear eyes with a merry twinkle, a perfect nose and flawless white teeth.

She was more than a beautiful face. Sarah is the first woman in the Bible whose faith we are told to observe. We know nothing of her childhood, only that she appears on the scene as the wife of Abraham. Her husband treated her as an equal partner, and she was the mother of Isaac, the grandmother of Jacob and Esau, and through Jacob she was the great-grandmother of the twelve men who became leaders of the tribes of Israel. Quite a woman!

Scripture: *Genesis 12:1-20; 16:1-8; 17:1-22; 18:1-15; 21:1-13; Hebrews 11:1-16*

HER SIDE OF THE STORY...

There is so much to tell, and so little time to tell it all. My life was full of adventures—some great; some not so great.

18

My childhood was wonderful. My parents were great people, and our home was filled with laughter, especially by my mother. She was one happy-go-lucky person, and some of that rubbed off on me. I learned to love life and laughed a lot. My home was a typical Middle Eastern home, but a refined one since my dad was wealthy. We had servants and all the goodies money can buy. Life was good.

In my teens, suitors began coming by to get a look at me, one who supposedly had classic good looks. Some of these guys were deemed to be prize catches, but none of them attracted me. I was holding out for the best! Then I began to see Abram in a new light. He was tall, handsome, wealthy and there was something outstanding about the way he presented himself. I fell head over heals in love with him! Incidentally, did you know Abram and I were half sister and half brother—we had the same father but different mothers. Growing up, he was just a big brother who was ten years older, but when I saw how all the other mothers in the area wanted him for their daughters and what a desirable catch he was, you know how it goes. Don't think this too strange because this kind of marriage was fairly common in my day. All along my mother kept telling me what a great husband he'd make. Mom was right! I told my dad not to let this one get away. I knew Abram would accomplish something great with his life and I wanted to be a part of that.

From the very beginning of our life together, he made sure I was an equal partner in all his business dealings. When we moved from place to place, my camel was always next to his at the front of the procession. This certainly was a bit different than in other marriages. I also discovered he was a man who had placed his faith in Jehovah God. He didn't worship idols as was the custom in our land. There's not really much more to tell you about our early life together.

Things really took quite a turn when I was sixty-five years old. I understand this is retirement age for most of you, but it sure wasn't for me. The first major happening that year was Abram's decision to move hundreds of miles south to Canaan because this God of his told him to move. The promise was it would become a fertile land for Abram and all our offspring. But did I tell you we couldn't have kids? Oh, we had tried, we had consulted specialists and finally accepted the fact that we wouldn't have kids. But this thing about the land belonging to our offspring did intrigue me. Another thing about this promise—it wasn't just to have a family or a clan, but we were to be the parents of a whole new nation, a nation promised to bless this world. How do you say "Holy Wow"?

Then the fat started hitting the fan! This new homeland wasn't so wonderful; we began to starve because of a famine. So we moved to Egypt. When we paid our respects to the Pharaoh, would you believe it—my loving husband and equal partner was afraid of him and asked me to help save his skin. He was afraid to tell this potentate I was his wife for fear they would kill him to get me, so he had me tell them I was his sister. (I was really a half sister, so this was a half-truth, I guess.)

Before I knew what was happening I was abducted by the Pharaoh's eunuchs. I was bathed, oiled, perfumed, coifed and wore a thin gauze-like scarf about my face and presented to King Pharaoh. Apparently he liked what he saw and added me to his harem. Immediately big problems ensued for the king—none of his wives or concubines could conceive while I was part of his harem. He called Abram for an explanation! Oh, oh! The Pharaoh decided I was the problem in spite of my beauty, so he sent us packing!

It may have been worth it because we made out like bandits—Pharaoh sent us on our way with a whole flock of sheep, cattle, donkeys, camels and servants. Oh, yes, and Hagar, who was one of Pharaoh's many kids through one of his concubines, came along with a bunch of servants and she became big, big trouble, spelled with a capital "T"!

And the same thing happened once again. This time it was King Abimilech who wanted me as part of his harem. I endured the same old embarrassing treatment until he, too, discovered the God we served had other plans for me. Like Pharaoh, he couldn't get rid of us soon enough. I'm spending too much time on background, so let's get on with the crux of the story.

God changed our names—Abram to Abraham and me, Sarai to Sarah. It didn't seem like such a big deal at the time, but I guess it was. Then three visitors changed our lifestyle, this time when I was ninety years old. They stopped in for lunch but what they said to us! I was cleaning up after getting their meal and couldn't help but overhear their conversation, especially when my name came up. They knew my name and said we were going to have a child! I began to laugh and laugh—me at ninety and my old, old man at one hundred! Absurd! I couldn't help myself. I even denied it when they confronted me about it! But this stranger knew I had laughed and said he'd be back in a year and his prediction would come true—by next year at that time, we'd have a baby in our house!

But we already had a child by Abraham, with my Egyptian maid, Hagar, and what a sorry mess that turned out to be! Sure, I was jealous! Wouldn't you be? To see my husband treat that woman and her son, Ishmael, like he did made me angry! You've seen this situation play out all the way down to your century—Arab and Jew, the big fight over who has the rights to the Promised Land. I could go on and on about this. My child and her child are still at war! Folks, I'm sorry about the way in which I was sure I knew better than God how to handle

His promise. But if you had to wait as long as I did, what would you do?

Well it finally happened that year I was ninety—Isaac was born! Did you know his name means, "God has brought me laughter!" And everybody else laughed with me, too. Imagine pablum and pampers at ninety! I encouraged everybody who came by to join in the laughter—what a wonderful one of your "sit-coms" this story would have made. Imagine, me a ninety-year-old mother, I kid you not, ninety and breast-feeding and diaper-changing. I was one happy, joyful mom! If *The Guinness Book of Records* had been around, I'd have been featured as the "world's oldest mother"!

But I wasn't always laughing, particularly when I kicked out Hagar and her obnoxious, ridiculing son! Served her right, but do you know that God came to her and her son's rescue and saved his life as well as hers?

I lived to the ripe old age of 127 with many bushels of happy, laughter-filled days. Even in death I was supposedly beautiful, but, of course, I wasn't there to have the last laugh then. Incidentally, did you know that I am the only woman whose age at death is recorded in the Bible? Pretty good, huh? I left behind a son and a husband who never forgot me, and I believe the world has not forgotten me either.

WISDOM FROM SARAH FOR 21st CENTURY LIVING:

Probably the most important life lesson Sarah leaves us with is: Don't panic when the promises of God seem like they are delayed. Hang in there and don't give up (of course, that's easier said than done). In due season, God who sees the long-range plan, will fulfill it better than you could ever do by yourself. Think of the sorrow and heartache and troubles (historically as well as contemporary) this world has been caused by the "Sarah solution."

Sarah

Let us also learn an important principle from Sarah—let us learn how to laugh and release the tensions of life. Lord, help us to trust You more, and have unwavering faith in You!

Chapter Five

DEBORAH

Desperate for peace in Israel

 This is one tough lady! Deborah lived in a day when toughness was needed. No pink ribbons adorned her. She was a woman who saw the big picture, and it was a vision of what could be. Her world was fashioned by political correctness, but her life was shaped by her relationship with her God. Yes, her position was unusual for a woman. Hers was the top position in her nation. In today's terminology, she was a president, CEO or prime minister.

She was desperate to lead her people out of bondage and idolatry. Her people had slipped and fallen and lost their faith and direction.

Scripture: *Judges 4:1-24; 5:1-31; Hebrews 11:32-34*

HER SIDE OF THE STORY...

You probably don't know my early history or how it came about that I became "The Judge" in Israel. Really, it was a "God thing" from start to finish. Growing up, I suppose, you could have detected in me a strength not found in most Israelite women. I was considered a tomboy kind of girl, and did I ever enjoy beating all those guys at their games! Really, they were push-overs. Maybe I overdid it. My mother told me more than once to go easy on them because they have fragile egos. She said that I should let them win at games and foot races if I wanted any of them to show romantic interest in me.

The only thing written about my background is the fact that I married Lapidoth. And what a catch he turned out to be—exactly the kind of a man I needed. We built a wonderful home together. Don't go thinking that he was one of those "hen-pecked" guys either—he was strong and not a wimp at all. But he was supportive behind the scenes. I never would have made Judge without him. He allowed me to become the dazzling figure I was purported to be. He gave me lots of excellent advice, love and encouragement. I only wish for all you gals out there that you will find such a catch to be your spouse. Yes, we had both good and bad times. One more thing, we had no kids, I guess so I could "mother" all of Israel. You've all heard about Jewish mothers, and I was one of them to the entire nation.

It's not often, but it still happens that a strong-willed and strong-minded woman like me bursts into human history to leave an impact. It's really very humbling to be used on the world stage. In my day, it was really unusual. But I understand other women have followed my example. England had her Margaret of Anjou who led her army over the country like a cyclone, tearing down tyrants and their kingdoms. France had Joan of Arc who led her army of 10,000 troops to victory to restore peace, although she ended up being martyred. Israel had its Golda Maier and England its Margaret Thatcher, and India had Indira Gandhi, so strong women are alive and well in your day. But I have digressed.

My courtroom was unique—it was under a palm tree between Bethel and Ramah in the hill country of Ephraim. I was the fourth in a line of judges who ruled in Israel. Did I tell you it was a "God-thing" that got me to this place? At first, the men were really worried that I'd be partial, especially to other women. But I was impartial and meted out judgments considered to be fair, honest, appropriate and thoughtful. It helped to be also called a "prophetess" or a person who hears from God. To be a judge you need the wisdom of Solomon, which I didn't have, but I listened to God. As word spread, the courtroom audiences quickly grew larger and larger. We didn't have "Courtroom TV" programs in my day, just great outdoor drama. My audience numbers kept on increasing until I was the best thing going. No other gathering came close to mine. I was at the top.

I became aware of the factors indicating we as a nation were facing a major crisis. I was hearing many of the same problems:

"My crops have been destroyed."

"My husband has been forced into slave labor for King Jabin."

"My daughter was abducted by King Jabin and forced to be one of his many concubines."

"My freedom to express myself has been taken away by King Jabin and his army."

"We were not allowed to vote in any of the elections past and those coming in the future."

"If I don't agree with this administration, I could lose my head."

"The edicts of the realm were enforced by the king's goons at the point of a spear."

The nation's soul was stuck on fear! You could almost taste it. Our land was in ruins because of this arrogant, tyrannical, Canaanite king who had an army of 100,000 men and 900 iron chariots. Every day before I ended a courtroom session, I would remind my people that our Creator/God was stronger than King Jabin and his general, Sisera. Those men were nasty and needed to be stopped. Because the odds were against us, the only way we could do it would have to be with God's help. In my vision for our land, I pictured us living in freedom from fear.

I looked around for a man to take the lead, but it seemed hopeless. So I drafted Captain Barak and told him to get an army ready; 10,000 men would do. But Captain Barak only saw Sisera's formidable army with 100,000 pairs of sandals on the ground along with enough weaponry to wipe out him and his outnumbered army. His raw recruits didn't really have a decent weapon among them—only primitive stuff like clubs, knives and stones.

But I saw our army equipped with spiritual weapons such as faith and prayer-power with God on our side, and realized the odds favored us! I saw the enemy as being totally defeated and wiped out with God's help. I knew God was more powerful than any standing army on earth, and I was sure He would fight for us!

There was a little problem—Barak, my hand-selected captain—was filled with fear. The only way he'd lead these troops was if I would go along. No problem! I was not afraid; in fact, I looked forward to the battle. Yes, I'd go along, and I'd lead from the front, not the rear, like so many generals have. I'd be the point woman! I was not afraid of 100,000 men and Sisera! Besides, I had the secret to victory—I viewed this enemy through the eyes of God. As far as I was concerned, our victory was already a done deal. Barak, however, was still a problem—I constantly had to keep after him to move it. He was a procrastinator. Finally it was time. I commanded, "Get up. Today is the day!" And so the battle began.

You should have been there. Maybe heaven has on file a CD or video of this battle so you can see it some day. God had been specific; he said to get the men from Naphtali and Zebulun and march them to Mount Tabor and specifically draw Sisera and his army to the wadi of Keshon. Then all hell broke...er, I should have said all heaven broke loose. Sheets of rain along with hailstones poured from the skies. Nine hundred chariots were stuck in the mud, panic ensued, and the whole enemy army ran away. Sisera abandoned his chariot and ran for his life too (I'll get back to him in a minute), and the army of Israel—10,000 rag-tag recruits—easily caught up to the fleeing and defeated professional soldiers. It was like shooting fish in a barrel. These soft professionals were easily outrun by the Israelite troops who had chased sheep and donkeys over the hills and were in top physical shape. The odds were ten to one—each Israeli slaughtered ten Canaanite soldiers until there was no more army of King Jabin. It was totally wiped out, except for one man, Sisera.

We searched for him but he had run to the tent of Jael who came out to greet the heavily panting general. "Come on in, my lord, don't be afraid." She gave him warm milk (spiked with a Mickey) and cookies, covered him up with a blanket to keep him warm, and just waited. Quickly he slept the sleep of the exhausted coward. This lady was something else. She took a tent peg and a mallet and placed the peg, point down, on his temple and whammo! One swing and she drove it through his head and pinned him to the ground. Gruesome, but very effective.

Then Barak came tooling up on his camel, and Jael flagged him down. "Looking for somebody?"

"Yes!"

"Come on in, and I'll show you the coward."

That really was quite a day, but Barak didn't get credit for defeating this overwhelming army. The credit came to me and

28

courageous Jael. The two of us were cut from the same piece of cloth—what a sister she was.

There's another aspect of me you might have overlooked: I loved to write poetry and compose songs. A day of victory like this deserved to be memorialized in poetry and song. So I wrote it, and Barak and I sang a duet, complete with back-up orchestration provided by the Jerusalem Symphony! He was a strong tenor; really he was pretty good. The music started off the celebration, and soon we were feasting on barbecued beef with all the trimmings. We celebrated one of the greatest victories in our nation's history. And I made it crystal clear—we had to direct all the praise and glory to God who had given us the victory.

Not much more needs to be said. You should also know that this victory gave our families peace for the next forty wonderful years! Thank you, Lord!

WISDOM FROM DEBORAH FOR 21st CENTURY LIVING:

Maybe you aren't an influential person with positions of authority, but you can still be a Deborah by encouraging others, influencing others for the good of society, challenging others to stand up with you, and showing them the way. You can be a real mother to your own family as well as a leader in your community. You can inspire greatness! Deborah stepped up to the challenge and so can you!

Her secret weapon was her relationship with her God. She listened, and she obeyed His directives. She learned to focus the wisdom and power of God in her world. She had faith that didn't waver when confronted with overwhelming odds. She was a victorious leader with God's help.

Chapter Six

DELILAH

Desperate to get rich

 Without question, this was one bad woman! We know very little about her, and what we do know calls for more questions than answers. We know she lived in the Valley of Sorek which ran between Israelite and Philistine territories. She had a home of her own, which was very rare unless she was independently wealthy or at the least a wealthy widow.

We would not be reading about her story were it not for the man Samson: the original strongman who was morally weak, the he-man with a she-woman weakness. It's always Samson and Delilah. They were linked in life and death. Victor Mature in Cecil B. De Mille's old classic movie, *Samson and Delilah*, said, "The name Delilah will be an everlasting curse on the lips of men."

Scripture: *Judges 16:4-21; Proverbs 5:20-33*

HER SIDE OF THE STORY...

I just know it—all of you prim and proper folks living in your antiseptic world of the 21st century absolutely despise me and all I stood for. Not very many of you parents name your

girls Delilah; you might go for Lila, but not Delilah. I understand; yes, I do. You see, I'm not a nice person, but it wasn't
always this way. Your scholars and theologians can't agree if I
was an Israelite or a Philistine. To set the record straight, I was
both—I had an Israelite mother and a Philistine papa. Keeps
everybody happy that way. It didn't happen often, but in my
case, it worked out swell.

When I was born my parents agreed that I should be called
Delilah, which means "delicate" or "the dainty one" in
Hebrew. A sweet name for a sweet little girl who was determined to grow up that way. Yes, life was good. We weren't
poor, nor were we rich. But early on I developed a real love for
money and all it could buy. Don't remind me, I know money
can buy just about anything except happiness, and it will get
one invited to every place except heaven. Let's just call my desire for it what it is: greed—pure, unadulterated, unvarnished,
ugly greed. That really was my downfall. I really should tell you
this little tidbit, my name, in Arabic, means "flirt" or "coquet-
tish woman." Need I say more?

When it came time to get married, I was concerned about
only one thing: to find a man with money who was willing to
spend it on me. It took a bit of time, but Mom and I finally
found him. He was nice enough, and he had lots of money.
Yes, he was old, but he had money. He was my sugar daddy. I
knew I could put up with him, but not for long, and the circumstances played out just right.

We had a huge wedding, a very long honeymoon and then
moved into this fabulous new home—my design, of course. I
smothered him with love, well, not real love, but a pretend
kind of love. He never caught on to the fact that he was
nothing more than a pawn in my grand scheme of life. It
worked—his love-making with a young wife soon did him in.
The death certificate stated he died of a heart attack. Okay,
draw your own conclusions.

I had finally arrived! I had a nice new home, new chariot with beautiful Arabian horses to pull it, a nice new fashion wardrobe, and servants. And did I tell you that he left it all, yes, honey, he left it *all* to me! No, we didn't have any kids to split the estate with. I made sure I was the only heir. And now, I was an independent woman, a quite wealthy independent woman, thank you. And, girl, I still had my looks.

I began hearing and reading about this superman in Israel. He must have been some kind of stud, although he made life miserable for my Philistine neighbors. He soon appeared on every wanted poster in every post office in the area. He made number one on the "ten most wanted" criminal list of the Philistine FBI. He was one mean dude and strong, too.

The headlines were something else: STRONG MAN TEARS LION APART LIMB BY LIMB...SAMSON CARRIES OFF THE CITY GATES...SAMSON IS JILTED AT THE ALTAR AND FLIES INTO RAGE, KILLING THIRTY MEN FOR THEIR CLOTHES.... They were really weird and exciting headlines. The *Israeli Herald* kept a reporter and cameraman assigned to him and his exploits. Oh, and there were more: ISRAELI LEADER CONSORTS WITH PROSTITUTE IN GAZA...SAMSON KILLS ONE THOUSAND SOLDIERS WITH THE JAWBONE OF A DONKEY... SAMSON DESTROYS PHILISTINE CROPS...SAMSON CATCHES AND SETS 300 FOXES' TAILS ON FIRE... And always the warning was added to the poster—this man was extremely dangerous. What a hoot it was to watch this little game of cat and mouse between Samson and the Philistine authorities. It looked like he could turn his awesome strength on at will. I really wanted to meet this hunk!

While I was on a beautiful white sand beach in the Mediterranean Sea, I finally met him. Suddenly a shadow fell across my body and I looked up to see this absolute hunk of a man. One thing really stood out about him—his hair. Never have I seen such gorgeous long hair on a man! He eyes were like burning coals staring through me. His opening line was, "My name is Samson...and your name is ...?" Not very romantic but to the point. He then offered to walk me to my tent. You don't turn down an offer from a hunk like that.

I don't need to tell you, this turned into a torrid love affair. Some people think we married, but he just moved in with me. Of course, word quickly spread. One day while Samson was doing his judgeship duties in Israel, I had some very unexpected visitors. Here were the lords of the Philistines asking to come into my home. Nervous about why they had come, I had my housekeeper serve them hot tea and sweets. They quickly got to the point, "Delilah, we understand you are keeping company with Samson. Is that right?"

"Yes...." I was really a bit uptight. What had I done?

"Each of us, that's right, *each* of us is prepared to pay you 1,100 pieces of silver if you can deliver him to us. Find out his source of strength so we can overpower him."

Honey, I tell you, that was serious money! In Israel a typical Levite might work for an entire year for a paltry ten shekels! A woman like me could live like a queen for the rest of her life on the reward! These guys were shrewd; they immediately zeroed in on my hot button! Who in her right mind could turn down an offer like this?

After consulting with myself for about 10 seconds, I said, "I'm your girl!" It was an easy decision for a woman like me. What choice did I really have? Should I live with this man who wasn't a husband and who could walk out on me at any time? Or should I enjoy the lifetime comfort of cold, hard silver that would keep a lady like me content with good food, fast camels and designer clothes for the rest of her happy life? Really now, what did you expect? Do you think I really loved this loser? I know, he was supposed to be this holy man and all. That was laughable. So what would *you* do?

At least give me some credit. I was up front and to the point: "Tell me, tough guy, what is the secret of your fabulous strength?" I asked him that very evening. It was cat and mouse, fun and games to Samson. He loved riddles and jokes.

One time he told me that tying him up with thin strips of leather would undo his strength. He laughed afterwards about this. It was an hilarious joke to him. I couldn't understand why he kept coming back for more! Didn't he know that I'd eventually wear him down and get the treasured secret from him? After all, I am Delilah, the dainty one with all the female wiles at my command. He was a dead duck from the beginning; it was just a matter of time. I didn't care if it took fifty tries; I knew I'd get him in the end.

After the third time, I was really getting ticked! He told his little lies about the secret to his strength, for fun. Three times were not the charm! Eventually I used the oldest trick in the book, "Honey, Samson, how can you say, 'I love you' and hold out on me like this?"

It worked then, and I hear that it still works today. It's clear, yes, I did whine and turn it on. And I kept at him—nag, nag, nag—to wear him down. Day after day at breakfast, lunch and dinner, I'd prod, nag, whine and nag some more until finally out popped the secret. Why didn't I think of it? It was so obvious—those seven locks of hair had never been cut.

He threw in the towel, and I knew it was all over for the big man! When he told me, I could see it in his eyes and in his manner—it was total surrender. I had pulled at the lion's teeth, until now he was toothless. He became a powerless strong man. It was over; he was pathetic, sad even. The fat lady had sung! I would now be a very rich woman.

All I had to do was put him to sleep. I must admit I helped

nature out and spiked his wine, just a little potion to keep him out. I tickled his face, ran my fingers through his locks, put his trusting head in my lap and out he went. Poor dumb guy, he didn't even see it coming. He had to really be out cold so they could shave his head.

I called for the men. "Okay, guys, he's out like a light!" And they took it all off; there was hair everywhere but on him. I shouted, he jumped up, they grabbed him, and it was all over. I cringed as they blinded him with a red hot poker. I can still hear the sizzle and smell the burning flesh; it was horrible. They not only wanted to capture him; they wanted to humiliate him!

Samson learned the hardest lesson of his turbulent life—the consequence of sin was separation from God. Well, I totally dropped out of the picture, and Samson did the work of a donkey, grinding out grain day after weary day.

There is a final line to this sad story. The Philistines set aside a day for a victory rally. It was to be held in the largest auditorium in their territory. I wouldn't have missed it for the world. I had a new gown commissioned for this celebration. After all, I was to be the celebrity star of the show and walk the red carpet. I spent time getting my hair and nails done, and face made up just so. I wanted to be there to join in the fun of ridiculing the man who was once the world's strongest man.

At the height of celebration after many rounds of drinks, the crowd was in high spirits. With a drum roll and a trumpet blast, Samson was paraded in and around the building to the sounds of the crowd's shouts. I'm sure Samson didn't miss my voice and my laugh. He turned his sightless eyes in my direction so I knew he heard.

I noticed something strange—all the while he was being led around the arena, his mouth was moving. He was led to the two main pillars holding up the roof and the balcony where he was tied up. Samson stood between the two pillars and about that time the emcee announced: "And this is Lady Delilah, who for eleven hundred pieces of silver from each of our reigning lords did deliver this Israeli strong man to be a captive!"

I stood up to take my bow, and it was then that I noticed his hair had grown out, not as long as before, but those stupid Philistines forgot to keep shaving his head! As I turned to yell at his jailer, I heard a shout of triumph from the lips of Samson as he pulled down the two middle pillars of Dagon's Temple and the place began to collapse.... OH...NO!! NOOOooo!

One final footnote: Samson toppled the temple and killed more than three thousand Philistines, including all their ruling class as well as Delilah, who left her fortune behind.

WISDOM FOR 21st CENTURY LIVING FROM THE LIFE OF DELILAH:

Money is not very good company. Delilah really didn't sell Samson; she sold her own soul and all this implies. She gained silver but think of what she lost.

Samson lived long enough to get back on track with his relationship with God because he repented. Delilah didn't live long enough to right the wrong she had done. And I believe the real bottom line is that God is a God of love and forgiveness, no matter how far astray we wander as human beings. Samson called on God one more time. And God heard and answered with a restoration of his strength—one more time. Delilah and her passion for money is a good example of when to turn desperation off and not let it motivate you.

Chapter Seven

JOCHEBED

Desperate to save her son's life

The name "Jochebed" implies the "glory of Jehovah" or "Jehovah is her glory." What a fitting name for one of the most powerful and influential women of the Bible! She is the very first person in the Bible to have a name compounded with Jah or Jehovah. How did she come to have been named like this? Did an angel visit her mother or make some kind of annunciation about her birth? We can only speculate.

She was born as a daughter in the house of Levi and married her nephew, Amram, and was both his wife and aunt since Jochebed was his father's sister. It's also believed she may have been quite a bit older than he was. Marriages with aunts, uncles, cousins, half-brothers, half-sisters and nieces were not forbidden before the giving of the "Law." Such circumstances were quite common throughout the Middle East. To this union were born three children: Miriam, Aaron and Moses, in that birth order.

Scripture: *Exodus 1:1-22; 2:1-11; 6:20; Numbers 26:59; Hebrews 11:23*

HER SIDE OF THE STORY...

From my earliest childhood, I always wanted to be a mother—not just any kind of mother, but a mother who would nurture her kids to become great and make a difference in their world. That dream almost faded away because, you see, I was a slave. In your beautiful world you have no idea how demeaning it is to be trapped in slavery where you have no rights. You can be bought and sold, abused, overworked, and beaten with no possibility of changing your circumstances. Life lived under such bondage is not a very pleasant situation.

However, we Jewish people had our ways. We made the best of our ghastly conditions. I married my Amram who was one of the most brilliant men I'd ever met. My mother considered him to be the best catch possible. It was a good choice; we made a good team and beautiful, brilliant babies. Life was hard, but life was also good. We still worshiped and praised our God and celebrated His goodness.

Miriam was ten years old and Aaron was a toddler when I became pregnant with our third. Talk about mixed emotions. I need to tell you, it had been three hundred years since Joseph died, and now we were under the rule of a new Pharaoh who ignored all the leadership Joseph had given to Egypt when he helped them survive a seven year famine. That's how all of us ended up in Egypt. It's a long story, but Egypt was good for us.

After a time, however, we had too many babies. The Pharaoh feared we would soon overwhelm them, so he made us slaves. Who do you think helped build all those pyramids and temples and valley tombs? Who developed the construction concepts allowing twenty ton limestone blocks to be cut from quarries, polished to within 3/1000s of an inch, moved from the quarry to be put in place, without mortar, to stand for thousands of years in a pyramid or temple?

Jochebed

My Amram was lead slave in his group. They'd be assigned projects to be completed in six months, six years, or in the lifetime of the Pharaoh. I remember him coming home and devising plans in order to complete these assignments on time. We'd pray about them; he'd wake in the night and quickly scribble something down and test it the next day. Brilliant solutions allowed these things to become reality. If we didn't get our tasks completed on time and within budget, heads would be chopped off. But where do you think our workmen, who later in our history built the tabernacle in the wilderness and the first Temple in Jerusalem, developed their necessary skills? The Temple was the most elaborate and expensive building ever built in the world! And we did it! But I've digressed. Let me get back to my story.

Why was I so fearful in my third pregnancy? In order to keep our population in check (but I really think he wanted to destroy us all), the Pharaoh declared that all boy babies were to be killed! Jewish mothers found all kinds of creative ways to circumvent this edict; it really was kind of humorous. The Egyptian midwives accused us Jewish women of being too vigorous and birthing before they could arrive and kill the boys when they entered the world. Finally, he said, "Kill all the male babies. Throw them into the Nile River so the crocodile gods can eat them."

You could hear the weeping and wailing on a daily basis. The crocs grew fat and lazy. Soon we were overrun with little girls. Then my third child was born, and no Egyptian midwife found out. The first time I held him, I just knew he'd be special. We named him Moses, and for three months I managed to keep him quiet and away from prying eyes. All my neighbors knew about him, but not a one let it slip. I prayed and Amram and I tried to figure out how we could spare his life. Amram shook me awake one night and whispered, "I've got it! I've got the plan to save Moses!" It was brilliant; it was a God kind of thing!

He told me to make a basket of papyrus reeds, cover it with tar and water-proof grease, and line it with blankets. Under cover of darkness, I gave Moses a hug and kiss, and, after feeding him well, I placed him in the basket and set him adrift on the Nile right in the area the Princess would be bathing in the morning. I gave some tidbits of food to Miriam, who was a very responsible little girl, to feed Moses when he cried. I had her hide and told her exactly what to say to the Princess. I knew she had pulled it off when she came running and shouting to me, "Momma, Momma, come quickly! The Princess wants you to nurse her baby!" Would you believe it? I nursed him in the palaces of the Pharaoh. Wherever the royal family went, I went. I ate the best of food; nothing is too good when a mom has to eat for two, you know!

More importantly, I taught this child all about God and about our history. The concepts of teaching and training children were remembered later by Moses, and he devoted lots of how-to-do-it instructions for our entire nation when he wrote the Book of Deuteronomy and more. I taught him line upon line, here a little, there a little, as we walked together. Everything became an occasion for teaching. This I was allowed to do until Moses was eight years old. I got the first and most important part of his upbringing! Then his Egyptian princess mother saw to it that he got the best Egyptian education money could buy until he was nearly forty years old.

And that's my story. No matter how desperate I was, it still took two of us, a slave and a princess whom God provided, to help him become the deliverer of our nation from Egyptian bondage. In so doing, he preserved the entire Jewish race!

WISDOM FROM JOCHEBED FOR 21st CENTURY LIVING:

Make it your priority to raise great kids! Especially protect them from any wounding during their childhood. Train them well, train them consistently and regularly so they get off to a great start on being productive adults. It starts in the womb all the way until you cut the apron strings and let them fly on their own.

Be bold! Be innovative! Don't be intimidated by your world, no matter how tough it might be. You can still be the parent God has ordained you to be. After you have trained your kids, trust them as Jochebed trusted Miriam in the most important action she was to perform in her childhood. This lady and her life and her actions are fertile ground for classic wisdom.

Chapter Eight

MICHAL

Desperate for prestige

There's no doubt about it, this girl was raised as a spoiled, bratty princess with a loud mouth. Her father was King Saul and her mother was Queen Ahinoam. She had an older sister who had five sons, but died prematurely so Auntie Michal raised them almost as her own. She became David's first wife for a while and then was given by her dad to Phalti the son of Laish of Gallim, so King Saul would enjoy peace with this neighbor for a few years. She was recovered by David about fourteen or so years later to be his wife again.

Michal (pronounce her name "MEE-kal" with a very soft "k" sound) is the Hebrew female version of "Michael." Even though she was raised as a princess, she seemed to have a lousy attitude. We can discern in her an inordinate desire for prestige and an indifference to the things of God. She also worshipped heathen gods. Although she was well aware of the covenant-making God whom Israel served, she still persisted in her perverse practices.

Scripture: I Samuel 14:49; 18:20-28; 19:11-17; 25:44; II Samuel 3:13-14; 6:16-23; 21:8; I Chronicles 15:29

HER SIDE OF THE STORY...

Hold on, I know what you're thinking before I even get started, "Michal was one spoiled brat as a child and didn't change for the better when she grew up." Am I right? Admit it. And I believe you have come to this conclusion because you, too, fell in love with the wonderful, marvelous, handsome, stud called David, my first husband. You just know he could do no wrong, so you blame me. Would you at least listen to my side of the story?

It's not easy being born into the family of a king. The court nannies, as well as my folks, all attempted to turn me into a compliant, cute, sophisticated little princess they could all be proud of. I hated those tutors! They were just ugly, old men telling me what to do! Always a nursemaid or nanny or guard with me—I could never get away alone! Sometimes when I was riding my favorite horse, I could out-run or out-wit them. It was a great game to play. Growing up was a real pain—wear this, don't do that, get ready, go to the party, dress for this dinner, and on and on!

It wasn't all bad. I don't want to give you that impression. I suppose I could have had any guy I wanted, but none were good enough, though there were lots to pick from.

David, on the other hand, stood out in any crowd, buffed to the nth degree, fabulous complexion, gorgeous hair, handsome face, already a hero as a teen idol and totally desirable. Women and girls swooned in his presence. Maybe most appealing was that his popularity didn't go to his head; he was humble—a rare character trait in a man so good looking. I ask you, "Have you ever really known a truly humble man?" See, my point is made.

He put down the giant, Goliath, with a single shot and cut off his head. He was a man who put fear and trembling into my dad and his army. It's a funny story...this peasant kid took on the giant and single-handedly defeated him and the whole Philistine army! The song written about him went right to the top of the charts on every station in Israel! They even played it in Philistine territory and the teeny-boppers went nuts and sang the song like they did in Israel.

Then my daddy, bless his heart, decided to bring David into the palace to provide background music. I learned he was a heavenly singer, harpist and composer, and I would sneak in behind one of the pillars to watch the show. Awesome! Then, you know what, I fell in love with him.

Daddy offered my older sister, Merab, to David, and he was so humble and embarrassed he turned her down. He told daddy he wasn't worthy to marry a princess. You want to know the real reason I think he did it? My sister was a dud! She was really the ugly princess. I think David had seen me. In fact, I made sure he had seen me. Merab was married off to some other guy, and they had five boys—bing, bing, bing—one right after the other.

Somebody told Daddy I was madly in love with this David guy, so he made a deal with David. He hated David so much and was jealous of his fame and his song that he really wanted him dead. And Daddy, bless his heart, knew what a problem I could be and used me for bait. I'm sure he thought that he'd kill two birds with one stone—getting rid of David and just maybe getting rid of me. I could always see through him—Daddy wasn't ever subtle. David said he couldn't afford my dowry since I was a princess. Daddy had already thought it through and told David the price for me would be the fore-skins of 100 Philistines.

Well, he underestimated David again because David killed 200 Philistines. It was disgusting; David came swaggering into daddy's throne room with this bloody bag in his hand, slapped it down on the table directly in front of the throne and proceeded to count them out, one at a time, all 200 foreskins and made sure Daddy saw them all. Ooohh! My dowry! Ugh! Leave it to my dad. You should have seen the look on his face! He had been planning on a funeral for David, not a wedding for us.

Nevertheless, we had quite a wedding, I must tell you. All the women were jealous, and all the men were envious. I was the star of the show. I really knew, underneath, that Daddy was using me as a pawn in his bigger scheme of things. But it didn't matter because I was madly in love with David.

David loved to go sit under the stars, strum his harp and sing me songs he had composed as worship to his God. We just weren't on the same page. Our interests were totally different. I loved him, but not his God. He loved his God and not me. I suppose I could have changed and learned how to play the tambourine or something. He loved to worship; I loved to shop. He loved to be with his army buddies; I loved dancing. We really had nothing in common except you know what, but it soon grew old. In about ninety days, the novelty wore off, and we really had nothing on which to build a meaningful life together.

Then I helped David escape from Daddy and his army. It was a hoot! But did my dad ever get mad and accuse me of not being loyal to him? No way. I was still Daddy's little girl, I guess. And David was on the run for years. I missed him. I really did, for a while, and then my love just seemed to die.

But Daddy, good old King Saul, had other ideas about what to do with me. He didn't want me hanging around his palace so he married me off to Phalti, who was some kind of royalty in Gallim, which was nothing but a backwater kind of place. I never had any feelings for this Phalti guy, although he treated me okay. He was a real wimp. I put up with him because I had to keep up appearances for my dad.

After about fourteen years, my dad was killed in action, and David was about to be crowned king in Hebron. Abner, slick Abner, saw which way the wind was blowing, and he made a deal with David to support him. Then David did something surprising—he told Abner the deal was off unless he brought me back to be his wife and queen. What an all-time mess this little procession turned out to be: Abner and me riding up front while pathetic, wimpy, heart-broken Phalti brought up the rear, crying the whole way to Hebron. Notice, I didn't cry. He cried, not me. I was ready for a new adventure. Poor Phalti, I waved as Abner ran him off and told him if he came back he'd be shot. My pride and prestige were on the line. After all, appearances count for everything! I was a bit embarrassed by this whole scene, but people soon forgot. After all, I was still married to David; there had been no divorce.

As for David, I really think his ego was at stake. How could the new king in Hebron sit on the throne while his wife remained apart with a weak, wimpy rival? It was politically motivated. David could not be seen as being weak in any area of his life. I saw through this whole thing. But give him credit, he was a perfect gentleman in public as he welcomed me back home. He kissed me passionately; yes, the fire could be stoked again, and said, "Welcome home, Babe! I missed you." Okay, enough was enough. The first night was fabulous, but then things between us soon cooled off.

You must understand that I was getting up in years at that time. I was no longer the ravaging beauty I was in our first marriage. Understand, too, there were more beautiful women demanding his attention. How could I, the aging queen, keep up with gorgeous Bathsheba and the beguiling and intelligent Abigail and the lovely Ahinoam of Jezreel? You need to know David had a real weakness for beautiful women. Over his lifetime, he accumulated twenty of them, some were wives while others were concubines, which is a kind word for mistresses. All the kids with all these wives drove me crazy, not to mention my sister's kids that I had to raise. No, honestly, I began to be an angry person. I didn't like the fact that rage was always rumbling just beneath the surface, and sometimes I couldn't help myself. I was really getting desperate to keep my place in the palace.

Come to think of it, I had lots of reasons to be as mad as a wet hen all the time. Sister, if you had been in my slippers, you'd be angry, bitter, resentful and desperate, too. King Saul was dead; David was anointed king and he needed to unite kingdoms so suddenly I had value again to David. No, not value as a wife, but like some kind of chattel to be passed around and traded from one man to another, all without my control. Now that I've said it, I'm really getting ticked off!

All this anger surfaced one day and finished what little feelings we had left for each other. There was something David wanted more than another wife; he wanted to bring the Ark of the Covenant into what we now called the "City of David." He did! And was it ever a serious wing-ding of a celebration. I mean serious celebrations! I watched this whole sordid event from a palace window. David had worked on the music, the orchestrations, the procession, the lyrics. He had redone, rewritten, and orchestrated it until it was perfect. I must admit that it was as spectacular a parade as I've ever seen. The ark was slow moving, and the dancers swirled around it; the sounds of celebration could be heard for miles. It was a spectacle to behold! Yes, I was concerned about what our neighbors were thinking.

The dancing grew more frenzied! Then my husband, of all people, joined them. In fact, he began to lead the parade. He whipped off his robe, then his tunic and all the other symbols of who he was as king and ended up wearing only a simple ephod that was nothing more than a tiny apron or loincloth. Absolutely disgusting—it was beneath the dignity of a king! I think, if I know him, he wanted to show humility and identify with his people, but he went way too far!

David had walked out on me, ignored me, left me with the other guy for fourteen years, married a whole bunch of other women, fathered lots of kids and left me out of his life until it was politically important for me, his first wife, to come home. This dancing business was just the straw that broke the camel's back. I was furious. The whole episode really turned my stomach. I wanted to throw up!

When I saw him finally coming home after the celebration, was I ever boiling mad! It was time for me to let all my frustrations out on him. When I confronted him, I was described as the "daughter of Saul" and not the "wife of David" and for good reason! Brilliant sarcasm dripped from my mouth with every word—even you can feel it in the twenty-first century if you read the account! There is no wrath like that of a woman who has been made to look bad!

I told him in no uncertain words that I thought he had acted in a most unkingly way that reflected terribly upon me as his wife. He looked like nothing more than any vulgar commoner in the kingdom. And in so doing he made me look like a fool, too! I missed the point, or so I've been told. David saw it as spiritual passion for his God. I saw it as nothing more than a disgusting display of fleshly passion let loose for the whole world to see!

He went from being happy and exhilarated to supremely angry in a nanosecond. He retaliated and the last thing he ever said to me was, "God chose me and rejected your father! I did my dance before the Lord! The next time, I will become even more undignified! You thought that was bad; you haven't seen anything yet!" Oh, was he mad! Here we stood nose to nose and toe to toe and our voices carried out through the valley—a royal brawl at the royal palace. Then, he twisted the knife another turn.

He knew the green-eyed monster when he saw it in me. "I tell you, Michal, those slave girls you despise so much will hold me up and honor me and will love me! That's more than I can say for you!" With that, he turned on his heels and walked away and essentially out of my life forever.

This is the very last you hear of me. No, he didn't divorce me—he just put me in limbo to live out a lonely life as a rejected wife. Really, nobody ever speaks of me again other than Samuel as he wrote this account. He closed my story with the saddest words that could be written about a Hebrew woman, royalty or not. "And Michal, daughter of Saul, had no children to the day of her death." Perceptive, this statement tells it all, the sad end. No, we didn't live happily ever after. Regrets? Yes, sister, believe me when I say that I lived with regrets and sorrow and rejection and depression for the rest of my sorry life.

WISDOM FROM MICHAL'S LIFE FOR 21st CENTURY LIVING:

Obviously, it's pretty difficult for a hot-tempered woman and a hot-tempered man to get along. In this case, it was not a small fire set ablaze in the moment of anger. When Michal let it all out, it was the end of their relationship.

When it comes to worship, we are to worship God in spirit and in truth. Michal had no relationship with God and therefore no desire to worship Him like David did. David showed us how to make our worship a total commitment. He set the standards in worship to the Lord; you can read his passion in the many Psalms he wrote.

Chapter Nine

RACHEL

Desperate to have a family

The story of Rachel cannot be separated from that of her older sister Leah and their husband. (We'll get to Leah in the next chapter.) Yes, you have read it right—these two sisters shared the same husband! However, he didn't love them both the same; the younger was his favorite. This family became the foundational family for the twelve tribes of Israel—one of the most important families in the history of the world!

Rachel was manipulated by her father and seemingly had little to say about the circumstances of her life as well as her life choices. In her life we see modeled many things, not all good. Her life was a real mix. She was the one her husband loved, but for many years she produced no children.

Scripture: Genesis 29-35; Jeremiah 31:15; Matthew 2:18

HER SIDE OF THE STORY...

My story really begins with my herding a flock of my dad's sheep. When it was time for them to drink, I brought them to our well. It was a favorite watering place for people and sheep.

Rachel

On this day, which began like every other day, my life took a drastic about face. This well was a bit of a problem for a girl, so I had to make sure there were other shepherds around—men, strong men—who could move the stone so my herd could be watered.

I saw three herds and three shepherds and knew I had arrived at a good time because I'd have lots of help. As I came up to the well, there was a fourth man, young, handsome, with a ready smile, and obviously quite strong. He took one look at me and my herd and rolled the stone away all by himself! Usually it took three or more guys, so I was impressed. Not only did he roll the stone away, he pulled up bucket after bucket to water my sheep. As he worked, his muscles rippled, and every time I looked in his direction, I noticed he was looking at me with a huge smile. He really was cute. All this attention was something. When he finished with the sheep, he moved in my direction, came real close, reached out and took my hands in his, looked me in the eye, pulled me close and planted one on! I mean, he kissed me—my first kiss—and I'll never forget it! My knees felt a bit shaky and something inside me went "flip flop." He held me at arm's length, pulled me close and kissed me again, this time with more passion! WOW!

He must have kissed me five or six times—it was heavenly! Then, of all things, he began to cry! This he-man cried tears. I couldn't figure out why he should be crying when I was so happy I could hardly contain it.

Then he told me he was my cousin—a real, live kissing cousin. His mother and my father were brother and sister. I didn't know what to do, so I forgot all about my sheep and taking care of them, ran all the way home and told Daddy all about him. I was so excited my words ran into each other. Daddy said, "Honey, just slow down and tell me again."

"He's my cousin, and he kissed me! Daddy, it was heavenly! I think I'm in love!"

51

And Daddy came with me to meet him—I didn't even know his name yet. Daddy gave him a big hug and kissed him. But this guy never took his eyes off me all the time he talked with Daddy. Well, I finally found out his name—Jacob. Best of all he came to live with us for a whole month, and he and I herded sheep together. What fun!

You'll never believe what happened next, but I just have to tell you. My daddy was always a horse trader kind of a guy and came out best in any deals that were made. It was "poor trusting Jacob meets the old master, Uncle Laban." I must admit my daddy was slick and had earned his nickname, "Lucky Laban." Daddy always kept something tricky up his sleeve, and he was shrewd. He had sized up his nephew real well and set him up. I listened to this bit of horse-trading through the tent flap.

Daddy said, "Jacob, you're my nephew, and it's not right you should keep on working for me for nothing. Tell me, what should I pay you and how should I pay you?"

Jacob got all nervous and embarrassed. He looked at the ground, then up at Daddy. I just knew what he was going to say before he said it. "Uncle Laban, I've been thinking about this already. I'm in love with Rachel, and I'll work for you for seven years if you will give me her hand in marriage."

Daddy didn't even crack a smile, but I knew him well enough to know he thought he already had the better of the bargain. He replied, "Okay, it's better that you should have her than somebody else we don't know." They shook hands and that was that. I had been bargained away, but I didn't care. I was in love with my love-struck cousin.

I've got to really hand it to Jacob—he stuck by the bargain. He said those seven years were like a few days because he loved me so much. When the seven years were up, Jacob went to Daddy and said, "It's time; I want to get married!"

Jacob...Jacob...Jacob. Poor baby, I should have warned you about your Uncle Laban.

It was an afternoon wedding, gorgeous, quite an affair. The bride was covered from head to toe, except for her eyes. Jacob looked longingly into those deep brown eyes and promised to love "me" for the rest of his life. Then there was a huge feast. Finally, night came and Jacob took his beautiful bride to his tent. All the pent up passion of seven years came pouring out in that night. But in the morning light, he turned to put an arm around his beautiful bride and discovered it was Leah! We had made her up to look like me, smell like me, and talk like me; being sisters it was easy to deceive the poor love struck guy. Daddy made sure I helped in this deception with the promise that he'd make it right, eventually. I was desperate to marry Jacob, and Daddy said that he would never let me do it unless I first helped him.

Leah is my ugly older sister—the Bible kindly describes her as being "weak eyed." When Jacob saw who it was that he had slept with, Leah just smiled at him. I thought Jacob would blow a gasket. Talk about being mad! He came storming out of the honeymoon tent and went looking for my dad with fire in his eyes.

He stopped in front of Daddy, and I thought he was going to belt him one. Daddy just smiled and calmly explained, "In our humble country, it's not our custom to allow the younger sister to marry before the oldest sister is married, period. Sorry, but that's the way it is."

Jacob stared back, turned white with anger, bit his tongue, and clenched his fists. He was dumfounded; he'd been blind-sided and never saw the sucker punch coming his way.

"Jacob," Daddy said, "you spend the rest of the week with Leah, and make the best of it, and I'll give you Rachel under one condition."

"What's that?" he spit out.

"I'll give you Rachel, and the wedding will take place one week from today. But you must promise to work for her for seven more years."

Jacob gulped, but give the poor guy his due. He was honorable in his love for me and said, "Uncle Laban, you've got a deal. I will work for seven years for Rachel because I love her!"

You can only imagine what kind of a marriage all three of us had. Jacob loved me, but try as we might, I couldn't get pregnant. God took mercy on Leah and saw she was unloved and opened her womb. Reuben was the first; his name means "Behold, a son." The second was Simeon; his name means "One who hears." Next was Levi, which means "Attached," and the fourth son was Judah, which means, "I will praise the Lord." I felt that each of these boys were named in such a way so as to rub salt in the wound of my barrenness.

I couldn't stand it! I screamed at Jacob in my frustration: "GIVE ME CHILDREN OR I WILL DIE!"—as if he could do something about it. We just didn't have any fertility clinics or specialists back then. So in my frustration, I told Jacob to make love to my maid, Bilhah! And you guessed it, she got pregnant and gave birth to Dan and later Naphtali. Finally, I got the better of my sister, and I gloated, "I now have two sons."

But you know sisters—Leah gave her maid to Jacob so he would get her pregnant, and she gave birth to Gad and a bit later to Asher. Then to add insult to injury, Leah got pregnant again and birthed two more sons, Issachar and Zebulun, and that's not all! She got pregnant the last time and had the only girl in the family, Dinah. Just think—she was the mother to seven kids and me not one!

I was desperate to the point of giving it up, but we kept trying! Finally, God took pity on me, and I became pregnant.

What joy! And Joseph was born—my first. And I really think Jacob considered Joseph to be his first real son, which caused a whole lot of heartache for all of us. I named him Joseph because it means "God has taken away my disgrace!" I was now a mother, and Jacob was a real father at last.

What a family we made. Not a happy family, at times. Talk about competition and jealousy. How could we not help it? But Jacob's God continued to increase our flocks and herds. And would you believe it—I got pregnant one last time and had Jacob's twelfth son, Benjamin, just before I died.

WISDOM FROM RACHEL FOR 21st CENTURY LIVING:

All of life is one huge test, and it seems these tests are given daily, mostly without warning. You would be wise if you didn't turn inward for your answers but learn to go to God for His answers. There is help for you and your home, your marriage, your children and your vocation. Since Rachel, the foundational concepts haven't changed.

The Bible is clear, "God remembered Rachel...." Had He ever forgotten her? No! When this word "remembered" is used, it's really an expression of God's love, compassion, caring and concern for His people. Remember, God has not abandoned you, nor has He forgotten you, neither has He left you without a support system! He will always remember you.

Chapter Ten

LEAH

Desperate for a husband's love

I've always felt sorry for this lady. However, the romantic story of Jacob and his two wives is quite appealing. The Bible certainly didn't mince words in describing Leah and making a telling contrast. If I had been Leah when this account was written, I'd have had some kind of protest. It says, "Now Laban had two daughters...Leah had weak eyes, but Rachel was lovely in form and beautiful. Jacob was in love with Rachel...." This "weak eyes" stuff is downright cruel. How would you like to go through life in the shadow of a younger sister who is beauty-queen material, especially if you were considered ugly?

I've often wondered if Leah had been at the well watering her sheep would Jacob have stayed with Uncle Laban? Because Jacob was Rebekah's son, he was also related to Leah as a cousin. This is some kind of story, so let's let her tell it.

Scripture: *Genesis 29-35; 49:31; Ruth 4:11*

HER SIDE OF THE STORY...

First off, I don't want any of your pity! Please, just look beyond the obvious. I know I never was a cute little girl or a gorgeous knock-'em-dead beauty. My folks and all the school kids and neighbors always reminded me of it. "There goes wall-eyed Leah. Have you seen bleary-eyed Leah? Look at her, beauty is skin deep but ugly goes clear to the bone. She has a face that could stop a camel!" I tried to ignore those hurting remarks. Before my life was over, I'll have you know, I dealt with this issue and managed to put it behind me.

Jacob was a love-struck naïve little boy when he came into my life—well really, my sister's life. To my dying day, I always wondered, but never asked, "Jacob, if you had kissed me first would you have loved me most?" I was afraid of his answer.

I'll be honest, honest as a sister can be—Rachel was a classic Middle Eastern beauty, high cheek bones, gorgeous skin, beautiful white teeth and a body that just didn't quit. The guys looked long and hard at her as she walked by. They glanced at me, but devoured her with their eyes. Whenever we went out, I let her do the talking and bargaining. She'd bat those baby browns and the men would turn to water, and she could direct them in whatever direction she wanted. Really, the bottom line for me and Rachel was that I did love her anyhow and was proud to be her big sister. I really taught her every-thing she knew. I was her nursemaid and baby sitter as she grew up. We did a whole lot of sister things together.

If you've read Rachel's story, I can skip a lot of details. You almost know all of my story, except my version. Jacob was madly in love with Rachel as were all the boys around, but Jacob nor any other of those guys would so much as smile at me. Not even a measly smile, although a lot of them laughed at me. So how was I ever going to get a man to marry?

Then Daddy made a deal with Jacob—he'd work seven years to have the hand of Rachel in marriage. It's like she was for sale or something. I watched the two of them with their plans. But I knew something they didn't. Years before Daddy had told me, "Honey, you will be the first one married, even before your beautiful sister gets married." I believed my daddy, but I never told Rachel and, most of all, didn't tell Jacob. Would he ever be surprised!

Seven years quickly passed and then came the wedding night. It was one of those boring Middle-Eastern weddings followed by seven days and nights of feasting. Then came the wedding night! Daddy had told Rachel, "This is Leah's night. You know our custom, you can't get married before she gets married. You will help pull this off; you will dress and disguise your sister to look and smell just like you. (This wasn't too hard; you see, our body types were almost the same and our voices sounded alike.) She will take your place."

It got dark and I was veiled and gowned from head to foot. After we exchanged vows, away we went to the special honeymoon tent. Jacob was wonderful on our wedding night! He was passionate; he poured out his pent up love of the past seven years! Girls, I'll have you know, I loved him and had loved him from the beginning, and I responded in kind. What a night! I'll never forget it as long as I live. He was a virgin, and I was a virgin. I was his first wife, and that was something I never let Rachel forget, either.

Then, finally, exhausted, we slept the rest of the night away. When morning came and the light was streaming through our tent, Jacob awoke and wanted to make love again. Then he saw it was me—Leah instead of Rachel. You should have seen the look on his face—anger, surprise, and unbelief all wrapped together! I have never seen anyone so mad in all my life! He blew every gasket in his engine! I thought he might kill me on the spot. He spewed his anger at me for my deception! He jumped out of bed, got dressed, and stormed out looking for my dad, who no doubt was expecting him at any moment.

Daddy was cool as a cucumber. I grabbed my robe and followed at a safe distance. He was sitting at the tent entrance, sipping tea and smoking his water pipe with a smug grin on his face. "Jacob, imagine seeing you here on the first morning of your marriage. Nephew, what can I do for you...please sit and have a cup with me."

Jacob was so mad he couldn't find words to express what he was feeling! Finally, he screamed, "What have you done to me? I willingly served you for seven years for Rachel, and you gave me Leah. Why did you deceive me?" I really felt sorry for him.

Daddy just looked at him with that all-knowing calmness of a poker player with a hot hand. Calmly he said, "Jacob, Jacob, please sit down...have a cup. You see, it's like this. I know that where you come from things are done differently. But here, it's our custom that the younger cannot get married before the older sister. Now just finish this honeymoon week with Leah. She's a pretty good lover, don't you think?"

Jacob deflated like a balloon. No, he didn't know that, and nobody, but nobody, had warned him. He was love-struck and naïve. He hadn't realized what a professional schemer my daddy was.

Give my dad credit. "I tell you, Jacob, in one week from today we will have another wedding and you can be married to Rachel!"

Jacob snapped alive! But here came the zinger, he was about to be blind-sided again, by my clever, diabolical father. (I had recently learned that his sister, Jacob's mother, was just like him. It must run in the family. I should have warned him.)

Uncle Laban leaned closer, "Jacob, we will give you Rachel, but you must promise me to work for another seven years!" He was selling Rachel this time. Talk about Middle East bargaining. Jacob, the poor sucker, loved Rachel so much he agreed to the deal. They shook hands and Jacob called my name, and we headed back to the marriage tent.

Jacob was all mine for the next seven days. In fact, this was the only period in our marriage, until Rachel died, when I had Jacob to myself. I made the most of it. And, according to my plan, I got pregnant. I'm sure it was on our wedding night. My first born, Reuben, meaning "Behold a son" was my delight. I just knew Jacob would love me more than Rachel, but it didn't work out that way. Oh, he loved Reuben, but I knew deep down inside, he was disappointed this son hadn't been born to him and Rachel.

You must understand, for a Hebrew woman, the very highest level of attainment was to bear a firstborn son with your husband. Sons were valued because they were needed to work the land and help with the family business. It was a disgrace to be married and not have any kids. And, yes, I couldn't help myself—I taunted my sister with the birth of my first three sons.

It was a bore—Rachel and Jacob got married seven days later and had another seven days of honeymoon. Two wives and two honeymoons in two weeks—believe me, he loved it! You should have seen the look on his face and the spring in his step! And I knew he would never love me like he loved Rachel. Which would you prefer—the love of a husband and no kids or lots of kids (seven in all) and no love from your husband? Ironic. You can probably guess what our home life was like. Every night the question was, "Who will he sleep with tonight?" You know, Rachel was never a really nice person. I think she was selfish, snippish, demanding and complaining. Don't get me wrong, she turned it on for Jacob most of the time, but around me and my kids, forget it! One more thing— she was sly, clever, a liar and deceiver. Not always, but when it suited her and her agenda.

Life went on, I was busy nursing and babysitting with four boys in quick order...bam, bam, bam, bam! Rachel turned green with envy! Not to be outdone by me, she forced her maid Bilhah on Jacob and said he should sleep with her. Wouldn't you know it, she got pregnant and birthed a son and quickly another son. Rachel said, "We're even...in fact, I've outdone you with my cleverness."

In retaliation, I gave Jacob my maid, Zilpah, and she produced two more sons! Then I got pregnant twice again! By this time there were ten little testosterone-driven little boys around. What a circus! Believe it or not, I got pregnant one more time, and finally we had a girl in the mix, Dinah!

By now, I was feeling sorry for Rachel. I had all these kids and my husband loved me for it, although not like he loved her. The reason I was so prolific was God took pity on me and gave me an abundance of fertility. This was to make up for the lack of love from my husband. My kids sure loved me. I was "super-mom!"

At last even I prayed that Rachel could have at least one child, and it finally happened! Little Joseph was born! Jacob considered him to be his firstborn, really ignoring all my boys. And did this kid ever become a spoiled brat! You should have seen the clothes this kid wore—designer this, designer that, the latest fashion right down to a many colored cloak! Really, this should have been the cloak given to the firstborn—what about my Reuben? No, it was Joseph all the way! The firstborn in Jacob's and Rachel's eyes. It was absolutely disgusting! Not a good way to raise a kid. And soon, he was really conceited. Spoiled was too mild a word to describe this kid. I could see that there would be big trouble ahead along with major heartaches. But Jacob would hear nothing of the kind from me.

Then Rachel got pregnant again, but the outcome was so sad—she died in childbirth. Imagine, she had shouted at Jacob, "Give me children or I will die," and actually she did die in childbirth. Her last words were sad, poignant, and prophetic. She named him, "Ben-Oni...the son of my sorrow." Jacob cradled him lovingly and named him Benjamin.

We buried her on our way to Ephrath; you know the place as Bethlehem. Jacob erected a huge monument to mark her tomb. I wondered what he would do to mark my tomb? Yes, we buried her but not her memory or presence. My husband was heartbroken and wept often since her death had been so sudden and came with no warning. Poor little Joseph wandered around like a lost kid with dark circles under his eyes from crying. But soon he allowed me to be his mother and finally accepted my comfort. Many hours we spent together when I just held him and sang to him and gently talked with him. Soon he was able to smile and laugh again. But squalling baby Benjamin was something else, I couldn't comfort him; he needed a mother's milk. Fortunately, one of our servant girls had given birth at about the same time and became his wet nurse, but I became his mother. It was wonderful to have little ones to care for once again.

But Jacob was inconsolable at first; his eyes became sunken with much weeping. I was now too old to give Jacob more children, but gradually he turned to my embrace and arms for comfort. Together we worked through our grief and eventually life became good again. We grew old together and really had quite a good time.

We moved again, this time to Migdal Eder for a spell and eventually went back home to my father-in-law. It was family time after Jacob and Esau forgave each other and made amends for their past. They were privileged to spend the last few years with their dad, Isaac. He was a really old man. In fact he lived to be 180! He was wonderful with our kids. It was such a good time, this multi-generational family. It was a time of celebration when Jacob and Esau were privileged to bury their father. His life had been long and fruitful.

Our story didn't end there—we went down into Egypt because of famine, but that's another saga. It's really Joseph's story. I was at peace with myself, my husband and my deceased sister. All in all, it was a good run of life.

History comes to our rescue with the fact that Jacob wanted to be buried in Israel. He made it plain to his boys he was to be buried with Abraham and Sarah, Isaac and Rebekah where ironically, he had buried me, Leah, the ugly wife in the grave with his ancestors. He insisted he was to be buried alongside of me—not his favorite wife, nor the wife he loved, but with the wife who was with him to the end—the "weak-eyed" one who really became the love of his life and a mother in Israel. Interesting how life turns out!

WISDOM FROM LEAH FOR 21st CENTURY LIVING:

Life may not have been so kind to you. You may have been raised with a beautiful sibling who got all the attention. But there is a fabulous nugget of truth found in Genesis 29:31, "the Lord saw (noticed) that Leah was not loved..." God loves all of his creations equally! But it's a real comfort to know that God notices us in our need, our rejection, our pain, and our desperation! My friend...take heart! God notices you; God sees you; God loves you; God cares what is happening to you!

Life is not over until it's over. Leah's life had the beautiful ending and not her favored sister. Leah, in the end, was the mother who shaped the life of her children as well as those of her sister.

Chapter Eleven

KETURAH

Desperate to marry a rich man

After his beloved Sarah had died, Abraham became a widower at the age of one hundred forty years old. Hagar had fled with her son to the desert of Midian, and Isaac had taken Rebekah as his wife and left his paternal home. So Abraham was left alone with his servants and huge holdings of livestock and wealth. But he must have been lonely. He thought about marrying again for companionship.

And that's what he did. Her name was Keturah—a much younger woman, a woman of child bearing age. How young? We don't know. But it was one of those spring/winter marriages.

Scripture: *Genesis 25:1-6; I Chronicles 1:32-33*

HER SIDE OF THE STORY...

Everybody knew about Abraham—rich, powerful, famous and, did I mention rich, really rich. In fact, he was the richest man in our entire part of the world. He was reported to have been richer than even some of the kings in our day.

His wife, Sarah, a gorgeous woman, was almost as famous

as Abraham. She became pregnant and gave birth to a son when she was ninety years old! Now that's something you don't hear about every day. And it was obvious to all of us that he was madly in love with her. Even when she died at one hundred twenty-seven years of age, she was a looker. This left Abraham alone and lonely. And what a fabulous "catch" he would make for some lady. One day, I thought, *Why not little ol' me? I'm not the looker Sarah was, but I'm young and still beautiful and never married. Why not?* The more I thought about it, the more desirable it sounded to me. He was without a doubt the most eligible widower in the world, and I wanted to be the one to catch him. But how?

To accomplish this mission would involve careful planning. I searched through my list of friends who might have known Abraham on a business basis, but there was no one who could make a proper introduction for me. Just how to let him know I was available would require a unique approach. But how? I knew a couple of things about him. I knew he had a good eye for pure-bred sheep, goats, camels, cattle and horses. He was a buyer and seller. I also knew he enjoyed walking through his fields, monitoring his herdsmen, and planning the next purchase of land or grazing rights. And I knew he enjoyed sitting at the entrance of his tent, drinking tea and entertaining the folks who dropped by to visit. But how was I to break into this circle of activity?

I got it! I had a beautiful classic-featured Arabian mare I had raised from a filly. She was well-bred with flowing mane and tail. She was well marked and moved with all the grace of her breed. She was trained to ride and had dropped her first two foals who also carried her classic lines. She would be my bait!

I had her washed, groomed, and her mane and tail trimmed. I even polished my silver studded saddle and bridle myself. Then I put on my best new designer outfit and, with a big smile, came riding up about the middle of the afternoon when Abraham was always sitting at the entrance to his opulent tent. Sure enough, he noticed me, and it was obvious he liked what he saw. Was he more interested in my mare or in me? I wasn't sure.

I rode up close so he could have a good look. He didn't say anything but took in my horse from hoof to ears, from nose to tail. Then he got up and walked around her, nodding all the time. He stroked her neck, and looked at me right in the eyes, and held my gaze until I got embarrassed. He spoke for the first time, "Is this horse for sale?"

I replied, "Possibly."

He invited me, "Please join me for a cup of tea, and we'll talk about your mare."

He helped me down. I noticed, even as old as he was, he was remarkably strong and well preserved—much better than I had hoped. He was in magnificent shape for his age or any age. I figured that the revitalization he was given by God when he was one hundred must still be in effect. There was a quiet, virile strength exuding from this man. But when he smiled, his face lit up, and there was a merry twinkle in his eyes. I decided he would be fun to be with.

He introduced himself, "My name is Abraham, and your name is?"

"Keturah," I replied.

Well, we never did get around to talking about my mare. We talked about life. We talked about the future we were facing. We broke the ice beyond my fondest dreams. It was beginning to happen. I was thinking, *I could fall madly in love with this fascinating man! In fact, I think it's already beginning to happen.* Time just slipped by and before I knew it, it was time for dinner and he asked me to stay. Of course, I accepted.

I was now quite sure he was interested in me more than my horse.

Finally, it was time to take my leave. He took both of my hands in his, looked me in the eyes, and said gently, with a smile, "I know we must meet again. Would you mind telling me where you live?"

"Of course not." He helped me onto my horse, and I made sure he watched me disappear over the hill. My heart was fluttering with the possibilities opening up for me. I know this was a bold move—something women in my day were not expected to do. Most marriages were arranged, and we didn't have anything to say about them because our parents did the negotiating. My father was unusual because he was understanding about things like that. He told me that he would never force me to marry any man. I think he liked to have me around.

A few days passed and I "arranged" another chance meeting just as an insurance policy. I didn't want him to forget about me.

I knew it would happen! Abraham's right hand man showed up at our camp, and he and my father were in deep discussion. I knew what it was about. My hand in marriage was being asked for, and the dowry was being set. This would surely set my father up for the rest of his life. Was he ever happy! As soon as Abraham's man left, my dad began to whistle, and he went to find my mother. But she had heard it all through the tent wall and ran out to give him a huge hug. Their oldest daughter was going to marry the richest man in the world! Preparations began immediately. Needless to say, I was overflowing with joy, too.

I'll not bore you with all the wedding details, other than to say it was a Middle Eastern affair to end all affairs. People came from everywhere to see this new bride Abraham was taking to be his second wife! The festivities lasted for seven days, and then our honeymoon took place. It was romantic and exotic. Oh, yes, Abraham got the mare, too!

Then something amazing happened! I got pregnant and gave birth to Zimram. You should have seen Abraham, the new papa! What a wonderful father he was! I loved to watch him hold and cuddle with our first son. Father and son bonded immediately. In my world, child bearing was the ultimate for a woman, and a man especially enjoyed sons. Abraham was starting over with his second family.

Oh, yes, I should tell you, Isaac and Rebekah approved of me and our marriage. I had been worried because I was younger than both of them, and to become Isaac's step-mother seemed awkward. Then, too, Ishmael and his wife and kids came by to pay their respects and gave me their stamp of approval because they could see how happy Abraham was. I loved him and did my best to be a wife in every sense of the word.

That's not all. I became pregnant again with number two, Jokshan, then Medan, followed by Midian, Ishbak, and finally Dedan. Six sons in all! We were one happy family.

Understandably, Abraham left everything to his promised son, Isaac. But while he was living, he set up each of our boys for the rest of their lives with a business. He helped them move to the east of us so there would be no conflict with Isaac and his two sons. He was very generous to them and to me.

Abraham died at the ripe old age of one hundred seventy-five! Unbelievable. He was still as strong and vigorous as he had been at one hundred. What a remarkable man and what a remarkable life he lived!

After he died, I never remarried, even though I had an opportunity. When you have lived with such a remarkable man as Abraham, I guarantee you will never find another one to match.

So I lived out my days as the matriarch of Abraham's family. I was surrounded by my six boys and their spouses and kids. God was gracious to me and blessed me as he had been gracious to Abraham and blessed him. So it was, Abraham in his later years was surrounded by a wife's love and care and a circle of growing kids.

Girls, this spring/winter marriage really was wonderful!

WISDOM FROM KETURAH FOR 21st CENTURY LIVING:

Life can be wonderful the second time around! Your life and expectations may not be up to other people's standards, but when two people are in agreement, all obstacles can be overcome.

It's never too late and you are never too old to experience a fulfilling lifestyle. This is the first such relationship mentioned in the Bible, and it obviously had the approval of God the Father.

Chapter Twelve

RIZPAH

Desperate for mercy

This is one of the most heart-wrenching stories in the Bible. It's at the same time compelling and touching. Rizpah, whose name means "a hot or baking stone" or "hot coal," was the daughter of Aiah or Ajah the Horite. During the reign of King Saul, he took her as one of his harem, a concubine. She gave birth to two sons, Armoni and Mephibosheth (not the crippled prince, son of Jonathan).

Rizpah is caught in the holocaust of national wars and treaties and broken promises. She is a pawn with no power of her own to act or choose. This whole episode came about because Saul's attempted genocide of the Gibeonites violated the terms of a treaty, which resulted in a three-year famine in Israel.

Scripture: II Samuel 3:1-7; 21:8-14

HER SIDE OF THE STORY...

To understand my story, you must realize one important factor. Women in my day had few choices. We were treated as chattel or sexual playthings or pawns in events over which we exercised little or no control. We didn't have any rights—couldn't vote, couldn't hold property—but we could birth kids. The more boys we produced the better. If the king wanted you, you had no choice. He just took you in spite of any protests you may have wanted to make. Your parents didn't dare reject the king, or they could lose their lives. It was as simple as that.

Growing up I was considered to be a raven-haired beauty. My good looks became the catalyst for my personal tragedy. One day King Saul laid eyes on me and said, "I want her!" He sent his right hand procurer of women to my house with an offer that nobody could refuse. "You have been selected to be part of King Saul's harem! Aren't you the privileged one? You will come with us, immediately."

I was spirited away on the king's camel and thrust into the harem chambers under the watchful eye of his eunuchs. There I was bathed, perfumed, coached, dressed and eventually I was presented to the King. He apparently liked what he was seeing, and into bed we went, just like that!

I quickly became pregnant and birthed a son, Armoni, who became a handsome young man. Soon, I became pregnant with another son, Mephibosheth. What a pair these two made—tall, striking and with lots of promise. They were great sons to make any mother proud. I spent quality time with them, made sure of their education, and helped place them in the administration of our nation. I knew they would never become kings, but they were part of the royal family. My parents certainly benefited because of my relationship to the king as did my sons. But that all changed in a moment of time; it was a senseless disaster.

I must take a bit of your time to bring you up to speed on the background for that horrible day. After King Saul and his son, Jonathan (the heir to the throne), were killed, the nation came under the rule of his second son, a weak man in every sense of the word, Ish-Bosheth. The real power was in the hands of Abner, the four-star general who led our army. Immediately, he wanted to solidify his power so Abner claimed me for his sexual playmate. Ish-Bosheth objected his taking liberties with his dead father's harem. He said it was disrespecting the memory of his father.

Abner exploded in anger and Ish-Bosheth, in his royal sandals, was too intimidated to do anything further about it. Of course, nobody consulted with me if I wanted to become Abner's plaything.

Abner took the opportunity, seeing how weak this king was, and changed sides. He made a proposition to David to deliver Israel and solidify the entire nation under King David. However, Joab, David's four-star general, liked neither this situation nor Abner, and killed him. Was I ever glad!

When David became king over a united Israel, there was a huge problem—the nation was struggling with a three-year famine. Finally, King David asked the Lord for the reason and was told that it was because Saul committed genocide on the Gibeonites in violation of their treaty. David called some of the survivors, apologized and offered them a pay-off which they refused. They demanded the highest price—blood! They demanded seven of King Saul's offspring so they could kill them. What they wanted was an eye for an eye and a tooth for a tooth. The fatal games played by people in power are something to behold.

King David was caught in a terrible situation—the famine would continue until this situation was corrected. I don't really blame King David; I blame King Saul for this mess. David picked seven young men—five sons of Saul's daughter, Merab, and the only surviving sons of Saul—my two sons, Armoni and Mephibosheth.

Rizpah

It was ugly—these guys had no warning, but were taken in handcuffs and led off by David's army and handed over to the Gibeonites before they knew what was happening. They screamed about an injustice being done, but it did them no good. Here were seven young, promising, innocent men being slaughtered to satisfy the human desire for revenge. Too many innocent people have died for the sins of their rulers in my day as well as in yours! I pleaded, but it was no use.

The day happened to be a fine spring morning; the sun was shining, and the hills were alive with the rising sun. I made sure I was there to witness this execution of supposedly justice in action. It was gory and inhumane beyond anything I can describe to you—these seven innocents were impaled on a stake. Their screams still echo in my ears. They didn't die easily or quickly. It took place on a mountaintop near Saul's hometown to be a reminder to all who observed. Then, their bodies were to be left there, to be exposed to the elements all summer until the time when the autumn rains would hopefully fall, signaling the end of the drought. The execution took place in late April, and they were to remain exposed until October. The Gibeonites were giddy with happiness as they exacted their disgusting revenge.

I did the only thing I could do. I spent those last few agonizing moments with my boys and then ran home to get sackcloth. I couldn't protect them from death, but there was something, meaningful left for me to do.

I came back with the sackcloth, lovingly carried it to the mountaintop and spread it over my two sons and took up my vigil. I beat off the vultures who came to pick out the eyes and tear at the entrails of the corpses, which they did to the other five, but not my boys. I beat them off during the day by screaming at them and hitting at them with a long stick. At night, I beat off the jackals that intended to rip the flesh from the bones and scatter the carcasses across the mountain top.

It was a macabre scene, I know. I kept my vigil day and night. As soon as I heard the flapping of vulture wings, I aroused myself to flail at them. At night, when I heard the growls of jackals, I awakened by my campfire and threw burning coals at them. It was exhausting. Some of my friends brought food and water for me since I wouldn't leave my vigil. Some even offered to take my place so I could get some uninterrupted rest, but duty demanded I keep at my post.

Friends said to me, "Rizpah, give it up! It's no use. You must get on with your life. Forget it." But I couldn't. I had to persevere. I was determined. This was an injustice, and it was all I could do to honor the lives of my sons. Yes, it was a weary vigil. It went on through April, May, June, July, August, September and into the beginning of October. I kept at it through long days and longer nights, through the cool of a desert night on a mountaintop and the burning heat of the summer sun. I would not give it up! Something had to be done to make this right!

Word of my macabre vigil eventually made its way to the throne room of King David. Knowing what we know of David's heart and possibly feeling reproach by my pitiful devotion, he took action.

I watched them come—David's men with David leading them to the top of the mountain. They lovingly and gently gathered the skeletal remains, properly wrapped them—all seven of them—and in a procession, we made our way down the mountain and buried these boys in the family sepulcher.

Not only that, David sent for the bones of Saul and Jonathan from Jabesh-gilead, where they were not properly buried, and brought them back home and all were buried together. It was a sad, but somehow joyful, day. My humble efforts paid off. This action of mine proved to be a pivotal point in Israel's history—the drought was broken; the famine ended.

Interestingly enough, the drought ended after the proper burial took place, not before. God answered with the rain. It seems that all along God in his mercy desired somebody to make a sacrifice to turn the tide. It just so happened to be me. It was through this long-delayed act of mercy and decency that the land was healed!

And that, sisters and brothers, is my story. It's a story of a mother's love, but it's more. It was a reminder to a nation that it is important to show love and respect for someone who has died. Also it's a reminder that promises made are promises to be kept. It's one of the building blocks of great civilizations.

WISDOM FROM RIZPAH FOR 21st CENTURY LIVING:

Even though a situation may seem to be out of your control, there is something you can do. You might be only one person, but in some way your voice can be heard. Don't give up when the circumstances are difficult. And always, because of love and duty, do what is right. The fate of Rizpah's nation changed because of her actions.

Persistence is a constant theme in the Bible. And the Bible also indicates that faithfulness will be rewarded. And faithfulness is all God asks, no matter what your situation. A God of mercy and grace rewards the faithful.

Chapter Thirteen

RAHAB

Desperate to change her lifestyle

This story is set in Jericho, a city that may have been the world's oldest. It had been established long before Moses led the Israelites out of their Egyptian bondage. In fact, it was considered the gateway into the land called Canaan. Just inside the city gates was a house of prostitution where the madam entertained primarily traveling merchants. Her name was Rahab.

In this story Moses had died, and Joshua was now ready to lead the Israelites, fresh from forty years in the Sinai wilderness, into the "Promised Land." But before they could move into Canaan, Jericho had to be conquered. Joshua, being the prudent military strategist, sent two spies to check out the place and that is the background to our story.

Scripture: *Joshua 2:1-21; 6:17-25; Matthew 1:5; Hebrews 11:31; James 2:25*

HER SIDE OF THE STORY...

I know what you're thinking as soon as you hear my name! "She was nothing but a common prostitute, a whore, and how did her story get to be in the Bible?" Am I right? Now don't go getting all worked up. I was just a practitioner of the oldest profession in the world, and in my world, it was a lucrative way to make a living.

How could I have done it? How did I become a prostitute? It was really quite simple. I had a very difficult childhood and needed to leave home as soon as I was able to do so. But how could I earn a living? The only way I could think of was to sell my body to the highest bidder and I sold it often.

But I also knew how to manage money. I saved, and then I invested it carefully. Soon I had enough set aside to buy my own place. It was a perfect location right near the main gate to our city next to the city wall. It had a window in the wall that came in handy more than once when a client had to quickly get away. I had a little rope ladder to accommodate this little maneuver. This escape route saved more than one marriage. Up until this time I had not married. I didn't trust any man enough to become a housewife, but more about this later.

All of this changed one day when two guys came knocking at my door, and I quickly let them in. They were obviously out of breath and sweating profusely from their run. I was used to strangers coming to my door, so I didn't think anything of it. They looked desperate, not in a dangerous sort of way, but they obviously needed help. They asked a lot of questions about our city such as, how large was our army, how strong were the fortifications, and when did the gates shut. My suspicions were immediately aroused, but one of them gave his name, Salmon, and was he ever handsome. There was something different about him. Finally, he told us they were spies from the Israelite army and needed to be hidden. What better cover than in a brothel where all kinds of men came and went at all hours of the day and night.

When they said "Israelite army," I immediately replied, "You're the guys who crossed the Red Sea on dry land! You're the guys who robbed Egypt blind! You're the guys who drowned the Pharaoh and his army in the Red Sea! You just defeated the two kings of the Amorites! Right?"

They admitted it was all true and told me that they were just camped on the other side of the Jordan River and were getting ready to attack our city. I had been hearing these stories from some of our traveling clients, and I was intrigued and fascinated by them. They regaled me with stories of their God who was more powerful than all the other gods people were worshipping. I wanted to know this God.

I said, "Come with me to my rooftop. I'll hide you under the flax straw drying there." Up we went and I covered them. I patted Salmon on the cheek, winked at him and said, "I'm not going to let anything happen to you! Trust me!"

Well you know how the grapevine works—word quickly got to the king that these two spies had come to my house. I knew it wouldn't be long. Sure enough the banging on my door happened. I opened it, made sure they saw a little bit of leg, and said, "Gentlemen, what can I do for you?" They were looking me over and finally one of them said angrily, "We know they're here, so bring out the two spies."

So I smiled and admitted, "Yes, they were here," and added, "but just before we closed the city gate, they left. I'm not sure where they went." That was as bold faced a lie as I've ever told, but they bought it and mounted their mules and set off in hot pursuit.

Then I ran upstairs to the two spies and said, "Guys, you have to get out of here. I sent them on a wild goose chase, but if you run to the mountains and stay there three days, it'll be all clear for you to return to your army." As I was about to let them down through the trusty window, I pleaded for mercy for me and my family. I told them how we were all quaking in fear because of them and their God.

Salmon replied, "Okay, it's a deal. We swear to it; you will be saved, but under one condition."

"Just name it."

"All your family must be in your house when we take Jericho, or they will be killed. You must hang a red cord in the window, and we guarantee that our army will spare you and your family." Feeling much easier, I let them down and sent them on their way with provisions for three days. I wondered if I'd ever see that cute Salmon guy again. He was really something else.

In four days the Israelites crossed the Jordan River. You'll never believe it! The Jordan was at flood stage, but just like what we heard happened forty years earlier at the Red Sea, they all walked across on dry ground! It was as though an invisible dam had been constructed, and the water backed up for miles. Tickets were sold for our people to stand on the wall and watch this crossing. We were absolutely awestruck. It was beyond belief what we saw. You can't begin to imagine the fear that descended over our city. What was going to happen next?

The Israelites set up camp at Gilgal, a suburb at the edge of Jericho in plain sight of all of us. They were 40,000 strong! We watched as they celebrated and worshipped their God—it was awesome. The officials in our city were absolutely scared spitless and did everything they knew to do to make our city impenetrable to their attack. We had these huge double walls, wide enough on top to drive a chariot around the top. Then there was a space and another wall. My house was built between these two walls. I wondered how they would ever overcome our defenses.

The next thing that happened was really strange. One morning, their army marched around our city. None of them said a word, not even a cadence was shouted—they were silent except for the trumpets. We gathered on top of the walls to watch. They just circled our city once and went back to camp. The next day they did it again! Why? We were really spooked. They did this for six straight days!

On the seventh day, they started going around the city walls at dawn. They marched around it once just like the last six days. But this time, they kept on marching. They circled us seven times. Then they all stopped. This time all the trumpets blasted, and Joshua issued a command we could all hear! "Shout! For the city is ours!" The trumpets sounded their charge, and the people shouted the loudest shout I had ever heard. It was absolutely incredible, beyond words! The walls collapsed and sunk into the ground, killing hundreds in an instant. The walls were so flat the soldiers simply marched in and began burning, killing and looting! The only thing left standing was my house. Talk about being scared—never in my life have I been so frightened. But all the while, there was hope down deep. I had never seen such a display of raw power. They had shouted to their God, and He answered.

My family and I were huddled, waiting for we didn't know what. I told them, "Just stay here! Don't go outside! The spies promised to help and save us." We waited.

Soon I heard a shout, "Rahab, baby, here we come!" I flung open the door, and there stood Salmon and his friend. I flung myself into his arms and held on for dear life, crying, sobbing, and laughing all at the same time! We were delivered! They led us through the rubble and to a special tent set up right by the Jordan. Salmon held my hand the whole way and kept giving me a very happy look. As I returned his penetrating gaze, I began thinking, *You know, this is the kind of guy I could spend the rest of my life with. He'd make a great father for our kids.*

We looked back; the city was in ruins and what hadn't collapsed was on fire. The victorious army was carrying out their loot. I was sad and glad all at the same time. What a day in history. Salmon held me tight and gave me a kiss. He insisted, "I've got to go back to my post, but I'll see you later tonight."

To cut to the chase, that night Salmon proposed. I became a convert and a follower of the God of Abraham, Isaac and Jacob—a follower of the God of Salmon.

After things had died down following the victory, Salmon and I married. This was something I thought I'd never do. Salmon assured me that God had forgiven me of my past, and he had too. My parents and brothers and sisters also converted and followed this all powerful God. It was a glorious happening. It was so sudden and a total about face for all of us.

I fell madly in love with Salmon and, of course, our first son was soon born. We named him Boaz, a real winner.

I almost forgot to tell you, Salmon was a prince—my real "Prince Charming." His was the magic kiss that brought me into a new life. He was from one of the most prominent families in his tribe of Judah.

My story is better than Cinderella's! From a prostitute to a princess! And don't miss the fabulous ending to my life's story, but someone else will have to tell you because it goes on for a number of generations.

Progressing through a number of generations we read what the writer, Matthew, penned: "Salmon the father of Boaz, whose mother is Rahab, Boaz the father of Obed, whose mother was Ruth, Obed the father of Jesse, and Jesse the father of King David!" And finally, "Jacob the father of Joseph, the husband of Mary, of whom was born Jesus who is called the Christ."

WISDOM FROM RAHAB FOR 21st CENTURY LIVING:

Although we aren't really told about Rahab's background, we do know how her story turned out. This story lives large with the mercy of God who is willing to take the most unlikely person and use her for His purposes in the big picture of things. It's a display of the love of God at work.

The scarlet chord is an object lesson of the shed blood of Jesus Christ that He has extended to all of us, no matter what background we have come from. God wants to take willing people, folks nobody else may want, to accomplish extraordinary things through them. It's fabulous, Rahab the harlot, became one of the ancestors of our Lord and Savior Jesus Christ!

Chapter Fourteen

LOT'S WIFE

Desperate to have it all

 The story of this woman is wrapped around the story of Abraham and her husband, Lot, the nephew of Abraham. The two relatives had separated and divided their holdings and land. Lot had been given first choice. Because of Lot's wealth and proximity to Sodom and Gomorrah, he was taken captive. Abraham then pursued with his army and freed Lot and the women and the people. We don't know who the women were, but likely they were his wife, daughters and their Sodomite female servants. Lot then chose Sodom as the area in which to live.

All we have for specifics on Lot's wife is a mere fourteen or so words in the Old Testament record and three in the New Testament record. But in the New Testament record, Jesus uses her as an illustration of the judgments coming upon this earth. So we are left with a whole lot of blank space. However, the record is such that there is much fertile material from which to make inference and fill in the blanks.

Scripture: *Genesis 18:16-19:38; Luke 17:28-33; II Peter 2:7-9*

HER SIDE OF THE STORY...

I'm one of those nameless, faceless and yet infamous women of the Bible. I was born and raised in Sodom with a silver spoon in my mouth and all the accouterments my parents could afford. Everything in Sodom and Gomorrah, twin cities of the ancient world, was overdone. We were addicted to the fast life, the materialistic life, the wanton lifestyle. If it felt good, we did it! It was a wicked place, but what fun! For example, our pagan celebrations were beyond description—public nudity, rampant homosexuality, blatant, in-your-face debauchery. Never, even down to your day, has a city lived with such abandon. Anything and everything was okay. We had no prudes around to spoil our fun. The conservative ones were all dead, buried and gone! Marriage and the home meant nothing. Incest flourished. Homosexual love was everywhere. Bisexual couples were the norm. Everything you can imagine and many things beyond your imagination were our playthings. That's my city! And I enjoyed all its sensual pleasures.

One day I noticed a new guy in the area—handsome and well built; he carried himself like he was upper class. He obviously enjoyed a wealthy lifestyle. He brought his holdings of cattle and set up his tent camp just outside our town. It was elaborate, to say the least. And it attracted lots of attention. Out of curiosity I managed to saunter out for a closer look. And there he was—tall, striking and rich! He had a rich old uncle, so I was told, but in his own right, he reeked of money.

It was obvious that he liked nice things—his clothes were all tailor-made and expensive. As I was looking over his fine array of camels, he mysteriously appeared and stood looking at me with his arms folded. I quickly became aware of his presence. I turned, surprised, and began to flirt with him. Immediately, he was intrigued and sparks began flying between us—you know what I mean.

He asked, "Would you like to take a ride?"

Would I? I had to be careful not to overdo it. I had to play hard-to-get so the excitement of the chase would be his. I replied, "Possibly."

"Which one would you like?"

"Makes no difference to me. You pick. You surprise me."

"Okay...how about that fine one over there?"

"Sure."

He helped me up onto the animal like a gentleman, although he held my hand just a moment or two too long. This one had a double saddle so he mounted up on the camel just in front of me and away we went. What a ride—the wind in my hair, a fast, racing camel under us, and my arms tightly about his waist. It didn't take long until Lot proposed and we married.

I knew something had to be done about our living conditions. I broached the subject on our honeymoon. "Darling," I said, "I've never lived in a tent. Not that your tents aren't luxurious, but it's a bachelor pad. We need something more permanent. How about a stone house overlooking the city? I've got some wonderful ideas, and I know a great architect and construction group. What do you say?"

Bless his heart, he bought it, and it became the talk of the town. Really it was a mansion, but I knew it was temporary. He didn't get it, but my next step was to move us back into town.

With my connections and network, a couple years later I surfaced a buyer who was offering a great price—a price too good for Lot, the Jewish businessman, to turn down. We sold our first home and built a really palatial one on the best avenue with the most prestigious address in Sodom. My Lot was a quick learner. I made sure he met all the right people. I must admit it—we did throw our money around a bit too much, but Lot kept on raking it in faster than I could spend it.

My next plan for us was that Lot should run for political office with me as campaign manager. With our money, we bought lots of votes. The first step was city council; in two years, at the next election, he ran for mayor and won by a land-slide. If there had been more time, I could have made him king over Sodom. So I settled for number two. I was more than Lot's wife; I was now "Mrs. Mayor," although I really pre-ferred "Madam Mayor." He and I were a great team. And that's how he came to be sitting at the major gate of our city, where the seat of government was in our time.

Two elegant, dignified strangers changed our comfortable lifestyle in a day. Lot spotted them immediately and guessed they were important and powerful men. He insisted they come to our house for a meal and to stay the night. They wanted to camp out in the town square, but no one in their right mind would subject himself to the possibility of homosexual rape. It happened all the time. (Where did you think the term "sodomy" came from?)

I was impressed by their company. There was something so different about them. I couldn't put my finger on it, but they exuded power and purpose. These, obviously, were men you didn't monkey with.

Now here is something noteworthy for all of you 21st cen-tury wives. Make a photo-copy of this verse and shove it under your hubby's nose the next time he brings home unexpected guests. Girls, here it is, larger than life: "He prepared a meal for them!" You like that? Well, here's also the reference so there can be no doubt, Genesis 19:3. Sorry, I guess I lost my head and digressed. Back to my story.

As we were eating dinner, all of us became aware of a com-motion outside that got louder and louder until Lot went to the door. The noise filtered back into the house—it wasn't a pretty sound. The men of our city were demanding that Lot bring out our two guests so they could rape them! I know it's ugly. And, at this point, I was embarrassed at the way we in Sodom lived and acted.

I almost forgot to tell you—together Lot and I had five daughters, three were married, and the two still at home were engaged. All five had made good choices among the best eligible bachelors.

Then Lot did something I never forgave him for doing! He offered our two virgin daughters to this lusty crowd to rape or do with them as they pleased. Imagine! I thought Lot was above this because he said he still believed in his holy God. I was angry and appalled.

But this didn't stop the crowd. When Lot was out talking with them, they stormed the door and would have taken Lot away except that these two strange guests were able to pull him back inside. You'll never believe it, but these two guys caused blindness to come upon all the men outside. The townsmen couldn't even find the door, although they kept hanging around outside the rest of the night! I've never been so scared in all my life.

Before dawn the next morning, these two men were shaking us awake and commanded us to leave immediately! We asked, "Why?" They said this place was so wicked it made God sick to his stomach, so it was going to be burned up and completely destroyed!

"NO...no...nooo," I wailed. I didn't want to leave our luxurious lifestyle, our beautiful house, my jewelry, my furniture, and my conveniences of life.

The girls and I began grabbing at things, but the men hurried us out. Lot went outside where the men who were blinded were still milling about and cornered our three sons-in-law. He told them what was about to happen, but they didn't believe him and thought he was joking with them. It was so sad. Why they didn't believe, I'm not sure, but I think it was because Lot was still considered an outsider, not a Sodomite.

Lot came back into the house, and it was panic time! These strangers had had enough, so they caught the four of us by our hands and forcefully removed us from the house. Outside, the hoots and howls began. Even though they were blind, they clutched at these guys and at us. These guys were something else, and then it dawned on me, they were probably supernatural beings—angels! The crowd parted and fell prostrate before us, and we walked right by them. Outside the walls the angels told us, "Run to the mountains! Quick! Move it! Now!"

Lot didn't look forward to living in the mountains with three squeamish females. Where would we go for toilets, for food, for mirrors, for clothes? He bargained with these two angels to let us go to a nearby tiny village named Zoar. They relented and said it would be okay, but not to ask for any other concessions. Then they gave us one more very forceful command: "Whatever you do, DO NOT LOOK BACK, or you will be destroyed with the rest."

Off we went. Lot was in front with my daughters, and I was bringing up the rear, as usual. I was thinking, *This is unbelievable—one minute we live in the lap of luxury and now we are like common street-people. I have been forcefully evacuated away from everything I love—friends, home, shopping, ad the good life. I don't know if I like this.* I fell farther and farther behind my husband and two daughters.

I didn't really know it at this time, but Uncle Abraham had been praying and bargaining with God to spare us, we who might be considered righteous. We weren't, but compared to the rest of the Sodomites we came off as saints. He'd managed to bargain God down to sparing the city if ten, only ten, were righteous. The ten were to be Lot and me, our five girls and our three sons-in-law and two prospective sons-in-law. Lot had managed to convince only me and our two girls, and reluctantly, we followed.

We were nearing Zoar when I heard an awful sound! We saw the sky blacken, and we felt the heat. Lot and the girls had now reached the little village. I moved slower and slower.

The urge began…I just couldn't stop it…desperately, I wanted to see what was happening. Yes, I remembered the command, "Don't look back!" But what would one tiny glance hurt? Surely nothing would happen with a quick, sideways, out-of-the-corner-of-my-eye kind of look. I quickly glanced out of my peripheral vision, and nothing happened. But I couldn't help myself, I needed a better look.

I stopped and completely turned. The scene was beyond description! Burning fire and brimstone was pouring out of the sky, and everything in Sodom and Gomorrah was burning and melting right into the ground. I'll never get that sight out my mind. Then the strangest sensation began happening to me. It started in my toes; they went numb. This feeling kept creeping up my legs. In a few seconds I couldn't move. I was riveted to the ground, my hands were going numb. I felt like I was about to pass out. Suddenly everything went black. My last thought was, *Why was I so desperate to look back?*

WISDOM FROM THE LIFE OF LOT'S WIFE FOR 21st CENTURY LIVING:

When God says move, we must move! When God says do not look back, we can't look. When God says run, we must run! These two angels gave clear, easily understood instructions, just like God's written Word does. Yet the family of Lot and his wife and his daughters hesitated as if they didn't really believe what was happening. They were so addicted to the materialistic life they were living, it was hard to leave it.

In bottom line thinking...stuff is stuff, and it's temporal, while living a lifestyle with Jesus Christ at the center is eternal. So what's really important? The material or the eternal? There's a problem right here—most of us like our stuff! But do we like it enough to lose eternal life over it? That's a question only you can answer for you and your family.

Chapter Fifteen

RUTH

Desperate to belong

 The story of Ruth is one of the most heart-warming and beautiful rags-to-riches stories of the entire Bible. It's interesting to know that only two books of the Bible are named after women—Ruth and Esther.

This story begins with a disaster—there was a famine in Israel. A family of four evacuates to Moab. Then the greatest tragedy that could happen to a woman in her day happened to Naomi—her husband died. The husband was the bread-winner of the family, and without one most widows plunged into dire poverty. This was compounded by an even greater tragedy in that Naomi's two sons died, leaving her with two Moabite daughters-in-law. Naomi became so saddened she changed her name to Mara because her life had turned to bitterness. It's against this background that Ruth bursts into our arena.

Scripture: *Ruth 1-4; Matthew 1:5*

HER SIDE OF THE STORY...

My reputation always proceeds me when my name comes up. Now, I was not always this kind, wonderful lady you know

91

me to be. I was raised in a place that enjoyed a rich and prosperous society. There was one major problem with all of us Moabites—we were idol worshippers. We worshipped the most bloodthirsty of the many gods in our world. Therefore, our society did not have a great respect for life. We weren't as morally wicked as Sodom and Gomorrah, but we were very sensual and sought pleasure wherever it could be found.

I was fortunate in that I was never selected to be one of the sacrificial offerings of children to Molech. Parents eagerly clamored for the privilege of raising their kids to be sacrificed in the fire as part of our worship rituals. Even though I was considered to be a beautiful child, my parents didn't totally buy into this ghastly, cruel and inhumane practice.

In my later teen years, I was exposed to something totally different and so wonderful. A family of four—mom, dad and two sons—moved into our neighborhood to escape the famine in their land. They were displaced people and never really integrated into our world. They were really different—nice people—but different from us. We all took notice of them.

Shortly after moving in, the husband died. We noticed the wife, Naomi, mourned differently than we did. Interesting. And about this time I began to notice her two sons—really sharp guys. My best friend, Orpah, and I made sure they noticed us and soon the sparks of romance were flying. She eventually married the younger, Kilion, and I married Mahlon, a real stud.

We later found out what a stretch this had been for our guys. According to their laws, it was illegal and forbidden for any Jewish boy to be married to any Moabite girl. Why? Because we were heathens and worshipped this horrid god of fire, Molech, and his brother god, Chemosh. But they married us anyway. I could never figure out the real reason why their parents didn't find them good Jewish girls from Bethlehem.

Life was good. Because their mother was a widow, Mahlon

and Kilion took good care of her. She stayed with us half the time, and Orpah and Kilion the other half. I discovered she was a wonderful lady and grew to love her. I could not have asked for a better mother-in-law. We had a great relationship. In fact, it was better than I had with my own mother.

Ten years passed quickly. Suddenly Mahlon and Kilion both became sick with some kind of disease about the same time, and to our horror, both died in a matter of days. The funerals were sad. I really felt more sorry for Naomi than myself. She was really left all alone in a strange country. Her husband had died and now her two sons were gone, too. We hadn't been able to even provide grandchildren for her. Now we three were widows. Our status was about as low as it could get in our society. We didn't have a welfare system, so the future for us was really bleak. We faced abject poverty and would quickly lose our humble home. You see, women in my world were not allowed to vote or to even hold property in our name.

One day, "Mom," as we called her, got a letter from back home in Bethlehem. One of her family members invited her to return; things were good again there, and the famine was over.

Naomi quickly made her decision. It didn't take us long to pack our meager belongings either. Early one hot day, the three of us started on the road to Bethlehem in Judah. We had trudged along with our burdens for quite a while until it was time for a break. Naomi was strangely quiet, which was unusual for her. I simply passed it off as her being deep in thought about what the future was to hold for her. Orpah and I chattered on, however.

As we walked over to our camels, Naomi took a deep breath and reached for both of us. She held each of us by the hand and said, "Girls, go back to your mothers. Go back to your homes. I'm too old to have any more boys, so it's useless to wait on me. I have no right to ask you to come with me to a strange place. Go home! You're free to go."

Immediately we hugged and wept and cried—all three of us had a group hug. Orpah and I both said, "No, Mom, we will go with you to your folks."

She looked at us through the tears, and this time was more forceful in convincing us to leave her, and we wept again. Then Orpah, thinking it over, looked relieved and said she would return to Moab. I never saw her again. I often wondered what happened to her; she had been a good sister-in-law to me. I was almost positive she had never really committed herself to following and worshipping the true God of Israel.

My mind was made up! I would not leave my mother-in-law! I expressed my love and commitment to her with a little speech. It just burst from me; it came from deep inside. I meant every word of it: "Don't force me to leave you. Where you go I will go. Your people will be my people. Your God will be my God. Where you die I will die. Nothing will separate us." So off we went, a young widow and an elderly widow.

We really caused a sensation when we arrived in Bethlehem. My mother-in-law had aged through her sorrows. Once she had lived well, but now she was clothed in nothing but rags. The people hardly recognized her because of the ravages of sorrow. She said, "Don't call me Naomi, call me Mara from now on because of my bitterness against God. God has not been good to me! In fact, God has afflicted me!" I must say she looked and sounded like an angry, bitter, aged old woman, but I knew her better. She was in a depression that I hoped would pass soon.

I still loved her in spite of her bitterness. Yes, she was tough to live with, always complaining. I did everything I could do to make life more pleasant for her. It didn't seem to help, but I didn't give up. I encouraged her to look on the bright side of life, but she rejected my efforts.

Our first concerns were about where to live. Fortunately, one of her family members offered us the guest room until we could find something. The next concern was about how to feed ourselves both immediately and over the coming winter months.

We had arrived just as the fall harvest was beginning. Naomi explained to me how their welfare system worked. Every farmer, when harvesting his grain crops, was to go through the field only once. He was not to harvest all the way to the edges or in the corners. What was left was for poor folks like us to "glean," which meant we could pick up what was missed or spilled in harvesting. And there was lots of competition for this subsidy. At times it got to be dangerous for a woman. Ruthless people could knock her over and take her grain.

The next morning before dawn, I started in a particular field belonging to a wealthy, rich guy. I kept to myself, a distance away from the other gleaners, and didn't flirt with the guys like some of the other women were doing. It was slow going, but by dinner time, I had managed about a bushel. It was not much, and we sure needed more. It was break time and I overheard the talk about this Boaz guy, the landowner, the very rich landowner whose field we were in.

Soon Boaz showed up and asked his crew, "Who is that young woman gleaning over there?" He'd noticed me! I guess I was still a looker in my late twenties.

The foreman had noticed me, too. He explained, "She's the Moabitess with Naomi. She's a good worker—only took one short break in the shade."

Then Boaz came walking over to where I was gleaning, stopped, looked at me and said, "Listen, don't go to any other farm to glean. Stay here and work with my servant girls. Follow the harvesters and take a drink from any of our water jugs when you're thirsty." I didn't know what to say so I bowed to the ground to gather my thoughts, among other things.

I stood up, looked him in the eye and asked, "Why? Why did you notice me, a lowly field worker?"

He replied, "I've already heard about you and the way you have cared for your mother-in-law. I know you'll be rewarded by the Lord, the God of Israel." And now, I knew something else was happening between us. I knew he was attracted to me!

At meal time he said, "Come and share my picnic lunch."

Then he gave orders to his crew, "It's okay if she gleans with you guys. Leave some bundles for her and help her in every way you can. Treat her nicely."

That night, I even had help carrying my grain home. It was unbelievable what I was able to harvest. Naomi was astounded. Then I told her all about this wonderful older guy who owned the place. "His name is Boaz."

Naomi said, "The Lord bless him!" Then she gave me that all-knowing kind of look mothers flash when they are on the hunt for a good mate for their daughters.

"Ruth," she said, excitedly, "That man is one of my relatives! He is one of our kinsman-redeemers."

"What does that mean?"

"That means, if he wants to, he can exercise the rights to buy the land Mahlon owned and marry his widow!"

I hadn't known anything about such a law. Life sure took an interesting turn. To top it off, I found out that Boaz was Bethlehem's most eligible bachelor. Yes, he was older than I was, but wealthy, handsome, well-connected and had all the makings of a good husband and father! Naomi was even more excited than I was. She hatched this little plan.

She smiled and laid it out for me, "Tonight, hurry home. Clean up, put on your best dress and lay on the perfume. He's finishing up his barley field. Let him eat and drink so he's in a good mood. Make sure to see where he stays for the night. He always camps out after harvesting. It's an interesting ritual. He does it to protect his harvest from any thieves. When he's asleep, bring your sleeping bag and spread it at his feet, and he'll know what to do."

I thought, *Mom, you really are the sly one.* I did exactly as she told me to do.

He woke in the middle of the night to find me at his feet. He asked, "Who are you?"

"I am Ruth, your servant. Please spread your blanket over me because I know you are a kinsman-redeemer to me." I know he was surprised and quite happy to please me. We talked the rest of the night through. The more we talked, the more I was thinking, *This is going to work for us!*

There was one glitch—there was another closer kinsman-redeemer, and he had first choice. Boaz planned to meet him in council chambers and before ten witnesses offer him first right of refusal. This man would have liked to redeem the land, but when he found out he also had to marry me, Ruth, a Moabitess, he turned down the offer, without even taking one look at me. Imagine! But I was ecstatic with the news!

Boaz proposed and we were married! Mine just has to be one of the most exciting rags to riches stories you'll ever read. In a short time, I was transformed from a lowly gleaner into the wife of the wealthiest man in Bethlehem.

God blessed us, and the Lord opened my womb for the first time and I gave birth to a son. We named him Obed.

Naomi was beside herself with joy. The other women shared in her happy moments and said, "You have a kinsman-redeemer! Now may your grandson become famous in all of Israel! How fortunate you are to have such a loving daughter-in-law; she's better than having seven sons!"

Daughters are always special. I felt special. The God of Israel was a loving and caring God. He was interested in all the affairs of even sorrowing, grieving people like me and Naomi.

You'd never believe what having a grandson did for Naomi. She became the doting grandmother. She absolutely spoiled little Obed. She was more than willing to babysit whenever Boaz and I wanted to go out for an evening or even when we traveled.

Life just doesn't get any better than it was for Boaz, Naomi, Obed and me! I truly give praise and glory to the God who made all of this happiness possible. There is hope when you place your trust in God. Don't give up on your life or the circumstances of your life. With God, all things become possible!

WISDOM FOR 21st CENTURY LIVING FROM RUTH:

This is one of the most fabulous stories of the Bible. It shows how your decisions will determine your destiny!

Ruth made a decision to bless and help Naomi. I believe it was done without any thought of a benefit for herself. But her decision to help and bless another resulted in huge blessings coming back to Ruth. She became the daughter-in-law of Rahab and Salmon and the great grandmother of David the king.

When God is your God and you trust Him enough to cast your bread upon the waters of life, you never know how it will come back to you. This has been another example of how our God delights in blessing His children!

Chapter Sixteen

THE QUEEN OF SHEBA

Desperate for answers

The term "housewife" hardly does justice to a woman like this queen. Arabic writers give her a name, Balkis, and Ethiopian writers named her Makeda. Take your choice because the Bible leaves her nameless. The Abyssinians claimed her as their ancient queen and even trace the descent of their modern day kings from a son born to her. So we can assume she had a consort and was married. Or, there's another tradition which says she and Solomon had an affair and he was the father to her son. These contentions are without biblical foundation, but they make for interesting speculations.

The country of Sheba is thought to have been located on the eastern end of the Persian Gulf—possibly today's country of Yemen. It was noted for its spices, gold, and fine woven cloth, and it was a center of commerce. Specifically its people traded gold, frankincense and myrrh to the kingdoms located in Africa, India and around the Mediterranean. It was founded by the oldest son of Keturah, Abraham's second wife, and joined together with the earlier Sabeans to form the nation of Sheba or Saba.

Scripture: I Kings 10:1-13; II Chronicles 9:1-12; Matthew 12:42

HER SIDE OF THE STORY...

I'm a queen and proud of it. I was born into a royal family and raised as a privileged princess. Everything about my life was focused on marrying a king and ruling as his queen, and I did marry the king of Sheba. You must understand that when seeking a king to marry, the choices are not many. He was a great guy and a fair lover, but a weak, wimpy, spineless, lousy excuse for a king. It quickly became evident that if we were to save the kingdom and preserve our positions, something drastic must be done! But what?

It was simple: I took over the reins of government and quickly got things back on track. I made all the decisions, I made all the plans, I cast the vision, I handled the administration, and my weak hubby was present for all the ribbon cuttings. Other than that, he spent time on his beloved boat running up and down the Gulf. He was nothing but a handsome, immature playboy. I did all the heavy lifting. He didn't mind one bit. In fact, he really enjoyed a lifestyle that allowed him his cake and time to eat it, too.

I was known as a tough, no nonsense leader. I was also heavy on the side of cynicism—you just can't believe everything you hear. You must know the source; you must investigate carefully before you believe. I was one of those gals who cut to the chase. No beating around the bush for me, just spit it out and let's get on with life were my philosophies.

Word about amazing things in Israel soon began filtering up to me, most of it from the Sheba Leader. But like most major "mainstream" media outlets, they were blowing this news all out of proportion. Not giving us the real story was their modus operandi. The headlines were outrageous, and most were generated from our foreign correspondents stationed in Jerusalem. Israel had recently burst on the scene and leaped to the status of a world power under the leadership of King David, and now under his son, King Solomon.

I just couldn't believe what I was reading! Solomon's personal take was estimated to be near a billion dollars a year—now this was when a dollar was a real dollar. Purportedly he had 300 shields for his personal body guards, made of gold. He ate off golden plates and drank from golden goblets. His throne was gold, two golden lions guarded it, and leading up to the throne were six steps on which were a dozen more golden lions on each side. The story was told that silver was so plentiful in Jerusalem it was just like pebbles on the road. Unbelievable stuff like that! But there's more.

He supposedly had fourteen hundred chariots, all trimmed in gold! There were allegedly hanging gardens in his dining room, and he had trained peacocks who pulled little golden wine carts from table to table. His servants were all dressed to the hilt in designer outfits. Maybe most outrageous of all were his wives and concubines. His harem numbered seven hundred, maybe even a thousand! No man could be that foolish or brave; I just had to meet this guy and see it for myself.

What really got me was the story about two prostitutes who both claimed the same child. One had to be a liar. So how did he deal with this potentially explosive situation? Solomon had ordered the baby to be cut in half—head to toe, so each mother had a half. Why? He knew the real mother would relinquish her claim in order to save the baby's life. Brilliant and very clever! I sure had a whole lot of questions needing answers. I made the decision to take the 1,500 mile journey to meet him and ask him the unanswerable! I hesitated at first because it would be 3,000 miles roundtrip by camel, but I ultimately decided that it would be worth it, so I gave the orders to leave in ten days.

Finally we were ready, and I must say our caravan looked impressive. Among other things, I was going to bring the man four-and-a-half tons of gold! *Not bad*, I thought, *this should get his attention, let alone all the other goodies I was packing.* Incidentally it took 45, yes, you are reading this right, 45 camels to carry only the gold! Why so many? A camel is good to carry about 200 pounds on a long trip and about 400 pounds on a short trip.

I must admit it, even I was pleased the way our impressive caravan looked. I wanted to make an unforgettable entrance into Jerusalem. First impressions are so important, you know. We were a spectacle as we made our stately way in through the gates to the city. People lined the tops of the wall for a look; crowds lined the streets. What a day! I wanted the buzz to go: "The Queen of Sheba is worthy to meet with the number one king in the whole world." I was proud to admit it; my presence and spectacle only added to King Solomon's growing fame!

The next day was the day for my personal audience with King Solomon. I was giddy with anticipation. From the very beginning, I was blown away with what I saw! I have never been so impressed in my life, and you know how cynical queens can be. The palace and grounds were beyond anything even I could have imagined.

Even more than the material things, I noted that all his wives were happy! How could any man keep one woman happy, let alone keep 1,000 happy? To me this probably was the most outstanding thing of outstanding things. Now in my country, women were considered to be equals with men, but this treatment of women by Solomon was above and beyond. The women of Sheba kept pushing and shoving for more and more rights. While here, they all seemed happy and content. I needed to know his secret!

In fact, I had brought along with me a whole long list of questions. Solomon was gracious enough to give me a private audience with him for the next ten days. Maybe in that time I could get them all answered. So I began firing away. He always made sense and answered every one of my questions and a whole lot more than I asked. I tried to stump him with riddles and brain teasers, and he solved everyone just like that! This man's mind was beyond belief. Never in my life had I encountered such a brain! He had created systems of management that really worked. His people were happy, his servants were happy, and the kingdom was humming and prosperous. I envied him and what he had done.

Then one day he personally gave me a tour through his temple. This was the most magnificent, most opulent, most beautiful, most majestic structure ever erected in the world. As you can tell, I run out of adjectives when I describe it. It was gold this and gold that—gold even covered the ceiling beams! The cost was beyond my comprehension. He said he had built it to honor God. Nothing in my world even began to compare to it, and I had seen some magnificent stuff. I had recently been to Egypt and there was nothing there that could compare with this—it would be like comparing coals to gold or grains of sand to wheat.

I was privileged to witness one of their celebrations of worship. Truly, I was lifted into a higher realm. The choir, orchestra and pageantry was incredibly uplifting and sent shivers up and down my spine. I was experiencing sensory overload. At times I thought I would faint dead away with pleasure. Nothing I saw or experienced began to compare with what I had been previously told.

I also must admit—now this secret is to be kept just between us—I fell madly in love with this guy! I can see how he collected 1,000 wives and concubines. The way he treated a woman was something to experience. He made women swoon; he had it all! He was movie star handsome, built like a Mr. Universe, with a vocabulary extraordinaire, manners that would make your Emily Post turn green with envy. He was gentle, yet he obviously had a strength that went deep. His piercing eyes exuded kindness, yet you knew he was like iron inside. He had everything and more to make any woman feel like a queen. He even treated his mother with respect and love. All those 1,000 mothers-in-law must have been delighted to have him as a son-in-law.

I've simply run out of things to say. My vocabulary is so limited when it comes to Solomon and his kingdom. To top it all off, this guy had the smarts to run the kingdom. He wasn't caught up in petty wars because he'd married into every other kingdom, and he was related to every king in the area. He was able to focus on building his people and their wealth. Even his infrastructure was fabulous.

To sum up this visit, at first I was ready to jump into his bed any old time. Even though I came on to him, he treated me like a queen and contrary to what some have written about us, nothing of a sexual nature happened between us. Sorry about that. No real juicy stuff to report. And I must admit I am glad because the wisdom he shared with me will stay with me all my days. If I can just implement a fraction of what he shared, my kingdom shall be forever changed.

Too quickly, my visit came to an end. On the final day, I brought my humble gifts of four and a half tons of gold along with gifts of frankincense, myrrh, precious stones and complete wardrobes fit for royalty. Yes, he was a little bit impressed, at least he acted like it.

I made my little speech, "The reports were true about your affairs and your wisdom. But I didn't believe them—you know how newspaper reporters are—until I came and saw with my own eyes. I must say that the half was not told to me. Everything I've seen surpassed the report. Fortunate truly are your people who hear your wisdom. And blessed be the Lord your God who was pleased to give you this throne." Solomon then stood and gave me a standing ovation.

Then he had me turn around to see the gifts he was sending home with me—it was everything I had admired that he had paraded before my eyes.

Oh, before I forget, one of the reasons for my coming was to work out trade agreements, a "NAFTA" kind of thing. It sure worked for us. As Solomon continued to expand his kingdom, he and King Hiram sent an entire merchant fleet to bring home the luxuries needed from my nation.

When I returned home, I was inspired to reach for greatness. I was determined to cast a new vision for my kingdom! To the day I died, this visit to Israel and King Solomon was the highlight of my life! My life and the life of my kingdom were changed by fresh concepts. I hoped and prayed that I could lead my people with some of the same wisdom of Solomon.

I also should tell you, he was upfront and honest with me. He told me the source of his great wisdom was a wonderful gift of God! And maybe the most important thing that happened is that I learned how to bless and praise the Lord God of Israel!

WISDOM FROM THE LIFE OF A QUEEN FOR 21st CENTURY LIVING:

To discover truth and wisdom in life, you must desire it and pursue it at any cost! The Queen of Sheba spared no expense in her quest for the truth. And, in return, she received the wisdom of the ages from a man who received it from God Himself.

Chapter Seventeen

QUEEN JEZEBEL

Desperate for power

Here she is—the real queen of wickedness. Look up evil, depraved, vile, sensual, or demonic in your dictionary and you will see a great description of her. In a survey of scholars, she was voted "the most evil woman who ever lived." Quite a resume. Her name means, "The Prince (Baal) Exists." How many mothers do you know who name their girls after Jezebel?

She was a Phoenician princess, daughter of the priest-king of Sidon. Sidon and Tyre, in the time of Jesus, were about the equals of Sodom and Gomorrah. They were twin commercial cities on the coast of the Mediterranean just north of Palestine. They rolled in prosperity and were the centers of the sensual Baal worship. She married King Ahab and reigned as queen in northern Israel about 100 years after David and sixty years after Israel split into a northern and southern kingdom following the death of Solomon.

Scripture: *I Kings 16:31; 18:4-9; 19:1-2; II Kings 9:1 37; Revelation 2:18-29*

HER SIDE OF THE STORY...

I was bad, completely bad to the bone and proud of it! I loved to flaunt it for the world to see! I didn't care what they saw just so long as they were looking at me. When you think of nasty little girls, put me at the top of your list. I was more than a handful for my pampered parents and mean old nannies. Anything I could do to disrupt things, I did it! I was the original "in-your-face" kind of gal. I loved to shock people. I did it all with a proud flair. Was I ever sorry? Never!

You get the picture? It's not pretty, but it's my story. It was funny when it came time to marry me off. My daddy wanted to get rid of me and discovered Ahab was needing a wife, and we needed peace with Israel. So I was pawned off on poor King Ahab. He never knew what hit him and never recovered. On our wedding night, with hands on my hips, in my most sensuous gown, I said, "Buster, let's get a few things straight right now!" You should have seen the look on his face. In no uncertain terms I let him know who was going to hold the power in this family and in the kingdom!

First off, this worship of their God had to go! It was so old-fashioned and restrictive. We tore down the temples and places of worship and killed every last one of the prophets of God! Ahab was aghast. He thought he might lose his kingship over issues like this. But I made mad love to him, and he got over his reluctance.

Fear is the weapon of choice to whip a nation into line, and I wielded it with an iron hand. I had my own hand-selected army and taught them how to be ruthless. It really didn't take too long before the nation cowered in fear. With these guys I made sure every symbol of religious worship was destroyed—no more posting of the Ten Commandments, no more altars, no more public prayers and no more mention of God in our courts. I turned this place into a heathen, Baal-worshipping country. Anybody who was seen or heard doing anything religious was to be killed. I made sure we got them all, especially their priests and prophets. Only one survived—his name was Elijah and what a royal pain he turned out to be.

We embarked on a building frenzy—the finest temple was to the sun god in Samaria. My gods were Baal, Ashtaroth and Astarte. Cruel and licentious rites were instituted. We had temple prostitutes and encouraged homosexuality. We wanted to destroy the average home. In order to do this, I ran roughshod over my weak, spineless, wimpy hubby. He was a mess, a blubbering mass of nothing. He knew he was in deep trouble because all these new things were sins against his God. Ahab's first sin was to marry me. Yes, it was a sin to marry anyone who worshipped idols. But I soon took care of all that. He didn't stand a chance against my ambitions and determination to get this nation on track with the latest fads of our day. I was one foul lady, but a pretty one with a forceful character, and he couldn't resist me.

No matter how good things were, there was this Elijah guy like a burr under my saddle. I tried to undermine his influence, but he still intimidated Ahab. I had 450 priests and 400 priestesses of Baal and Asherah along with their temples. Their worship was fun and mesmerizing at the same time. We encouraged rampant sexual immorality, temple prostitution with male and female prostitutes and even child sacrifices! It was me and not Ahab who gave the orders to put all these things in place.

Now don't go jumping to the conclusion that I was the only one who was wicked. Ahab wasn't exactly an angel, either. Once he got started, with my help, he was more evil than all the other kings before him combined, and that's saying something! I enjoyed every minute of it. People have blamed me for how bad he became, but a whole lot was his own doing, you understand.

Ahab hesitated about killing off the prophets of God, so I gave this order, too. If it took murdering all these guys, so what? Anything to control and institute a whole new society and way of worship. Removing their religious foundations was critical to the success of my plans. I have proudly worn the title of "The Lady MacBeth of the Bible."

Elijah turned up the heat under poor Ahab! I thought Ahab would crumble, but I helped him buck up. Poor guy, he was a nervous twit. Elijah challenged him, "Let's settle this once and for all. Let's see whose god is the most powerful." The ground rules were simple—all 850 of our prophets were to climb Mt. Carmel with Elijah where they would build two altars and prepare two bulls for a sacrifice. The god who set the sacrifice on fire (no matches allowed) would be the god we would serve. Ahab and I thought it a great plan.

It turned out to be the spectacle of all spectacles! I told Ahab I didn't need to attend because our side would win hands down. The odds were 850 to 1. Ahab didn't want to miss this—it was your World Series and Super Bowl all wrapped up in one. You know how guys and games are. I didn't need the aggravation nor did I want to trudge up the side of the scrawny mountain. So I had to depend on Ahab's play-by-play account.

When Ahab came home that night, I immediately detected he was in a real funk. I'd never seen him so whipped like a puppy dog with his tail between his legs.

"Tell me!" I said.

It seems that after the efforts of our prophets proved futile, Elijah held up his hands for silence. He dramatically turned his face toward heaven and prayed a simple thirty-second prayer. What happened next scared the wittles out of old Ahab.

Whooosshhh! Bam! Crackle! Pop! Talk about loud, powerful, unbelievable noise! Fire came out of the blue like a lightning strike and burned up not only the sacrifice, but also the firewood, which he had doused with water, the stones that made up the altar, and the water in the trench surrounding it. It left a huge hole on top of the mountain.

The people all bowed on the ground in awe of their God! Then they shouted, "The Lord, He is God!" and Ahab said that this went on for what seemed like hours. Then Elijah had all 850 of our guys killed! Right there! Right then! Right in front of all the people.

I was furious at Elijah and at Ahab's complete incompetence to deal with him. I summoned a messenger and told him to immediately find that so-called prophet and tell him by this time tomorrow he would be pushing up daisies and eating dirt!

You know what happened? Elijah ran for his life! I guess I showed him who is really boss. But Baal worship was dead. Imagine the power of this one man to overthrow my popular movement and move our nation to the extreme right. I'm still mad every time I think about it. If it was the last thing I did, I wanted to kill that man and do away with the worship of his God! But Elijah just dropped out of sight.

Time went on. Then one day I came home to find my weak, wimpy king in a real funk. He sat on his bed, pouting like a little kid.

Standing with my arms folded in front of me, I said, "Big boy...what's your problem, now?"

It was nothing but a little vineyard, just a piece of land he wanted, but Naboth had refused to sell it to him. Somebody needed to put some spine into the guy; after all, he was the king with unlimited power. Have Naboth killed! It was an easy fix. Ahab wanted the land, but he didn't want to do the dirty work.

It was so easy; I set Naboth up. At a banquet I paid off a couple of informers who perjured themselves against Naboth who ended up being stoned as a result. Just like that, the vineyard was his. "Now get off your duff and act like a man," I told him.

But Elijah, after a three-year absence, came back from his wilderness safari. He had gotten over his fear of me somehow. He confronted Ahab in his new vineyard and told him he was a dead man and that I would die a horrible, gory death. Ahab really fell into a black depression and acted like a baby.

Elijah made me mad. No man was going to threaten me. No man could intimidate me. He had predicted dogs would eat me. Ha! Dogs to eat a queen, laughable! Elijah is just a mean old man who wants revenge. I laughed it off but not Ahab. I tell you, Ahab became so scared he tore his clothes, put on sackcloth, fasted, and of all things, he humbled himself before his God. Imagine! Elijah said this act postponed judgment on Ahab, but it would be carried out on his house in the next generation. Not me! I'm not going about in sackcloth and humbling myself. It was unbelievable what Ahab did, but you'll never see this gal groveling to God or anybody else.

In the next battle, a stray arrow found a chink in Ahab's beautiful, handmade, custom-tailored armor even though he was in disguise. I guess that's how the royal cookie crumbled. Dead just like that! I made sure he had a royal funeral, poor baby. But now it was my turn to be completely in charge! Nobody was happy with a queen totally in charge, but I took no guff from anybody. I was vicious in enforcing my rule. I really shaped up the troops. This went on for ten years. I hated God but loved my Baal and his sexy worship. What a ride it was with me in the driver's seat!

One day, through my well-developed grapevine, I heard about this Jehu guy. I just had a nagging sense some things were not quite right when my sources said, "God has chosen Jehu as the next king." Not good—something drastic must be done. Even more disconcerting, the local media reported that not only was Jehu to be king, but his first mission was to destroy the house of Ahab!

With that news, I hate to admit it, I became a little afraid because their God could do some weird things. The spectacle of fire coming down from heaven was too much in my mind. I lost some sleep over this situation, I have to admit. I sacrificed and called on my gods for protection. Eventually I heard the great news that Elijah had disappeared. Witnesses said it was a chariot of fire coming to take him home. It got front page news for days. Some fairy tale that was. But what really mattered, he was gone! Did I ever throw a party to celebrate! And if he's gone, his predictions were also gone, or so I thought.

Some time after this wonderful news, one of my spies broke the news to me, "Jehu is coming to town." I looked out my top window, and I could see the dust cloud he was raising.

I rushed to put on my paint and powder and my most sexy dress. I rushed over and planted my pretty self high in the castle window to watch him come. Finally, he was there right beneath my window in the open courtyard. I smiled, undaunted, because I was quite capable of controlling men, and I was sure Jehu would be just another push-over.

He stopped, looked up, and with all the sarcasm I could muster, I hurled the vilest insult I could at him. I called him "Zimri." Zimri was the nastiest insult you could call a man in my day. I was not one bit afraid. I had never backed down from a challenge. I'd take care of this little pipsqueak who fancied himself the next king! I shouted, "Have you come to make peace with me, you Zimri—you, who murdered your king!" I quickly shouted the order for my personal guard to arrest and kill Jehu.

He shouted up, "Who is on my side?"

What impudence! He didn't even address me, the queen. Two or three of my most trusted eunuchs looked out the window at Jehu. I saw the look on their faces and immediately knew what they were thinking, *For thirty years we have been or-*

dered about, humiliated and beaten by this witchy queen, here's our chance! It took them about two seconds to make their decision!

They grabbed me, and I screamed at them, "Who do you think you are? I'll have you killed for touching me!"

Jehu shouted up at those guys, "Throw her down!"

I screamed and scratched; it was such a long way down. They threw me out of the upper chamber window. I was screaming, "You can't do this to me...I'm the quueeee..."

Justice was swift and deadly! Her blood splattered on the wall and the horses as they trampled her. Lost your appetite? Not Jehu. The gore didn't bother him because he walked into the palace and had a nice lunch. He may have thought afterwards, *Really, Jezebel was a queen, perhaps we should at least give her a burial.* So Jehu ordered some of his guys to give her a proper burial. In the meantime, the wild dogs made a feast of her carcass, and all they found of her remains was a skull, her hands and her feet.

WISDOM FROM THE LIFE OF JEZEBEL FOR 21st CENTURY LIVING:

At her end, her body was nothing more than a piece of garbage, barely enough to bury. Yes, it's a vivid, horrible story of a wasted, wanton life lived in the fast lane. It was selfish ambition carried out to the bitter end.

It's a hard lesson, but one we all must take heed to acknowledge. You cannot mock God and get away with it forever! If you do not meet judgment in this life, you will positively face judgment in the life to come. God gives grace and mercy to the humble, but for the haughty and proud, there is nothing but doom and damnation.

Even Ahab, whom the Bible says was more wicked and vile than any other king before him, received mercy from God when he humbled himself, put on sackcloth and fasted.

Chapter Eighteen

THE WIDOW OF ZAREPHATH

Desperate to survive

Zarephath was a very small town whose only claim to fame is that the prophet Elijah hid in a widow's home there for about two years or more. It was a very small town somewhere on the Mediterranean Sea coast between Tyre and Sidon. Elijah was in hiding because of the price placed on his head, dead or alive, by the wicked Queen Jezebel, his arch-enemy. He had been living along a creek and was fed by the ravens. The famine lasted so long the creek dried up, and Elijah was sent by God to a widow in Zarephath.

This widow was a Phoenician who lived in a society which treated widows strictly as second-class citizens. There was no safety net for them as there was for neighboring Israelite widows. Here, she was strictly left alone to her own devices. If she died, no one would have paid any attention. This gives us a bit of background against which this story unfolds.

Scripture: I Kings 17:8-24; Luke 4:25-26

HER SIDE OF THIS STORY...

I will always remember this day as long as I live! It really was planned to be my last day with something to eat. It wasn't much, just a simple little cake to share between my son and me. Maybe I'm getting a bit ahead of myself. Before I continue, I will show you why and how I came to such desperate straits.

I was born a Phoenician. The heathen culture in which I was raised should tell you a whole lot about me. Like all good Phoenician girls, my childhood had only one focus—preparation on how to catch a good husband and be a good wife, mother and cook. I met these goals, not quite in that order. Thankfully, I did catch a wonderful man, and he was a good provider. Together we had just one child, a good son. I wasn't too good at the cooking thing, especially in the beginning, but I did improve. However, I was an excellent mother, if I have to say so myself. The three of us did enjoy a good life.

One day, my husband went off to work as usual, giving me a kiss and a hug to our handsome and growing son. He worked in the local sawmill; it was a good-paying job. Late in the afternoon, his boss knocked on our door—this was his first visit, and it was very unusual. Why was he here? What had happened? I was immediately alarmed.

He said, "Please sit down. I'm sorry to tell you, but your husband has just been killed in a tragic accident. One of the logs he was working on slipped and fell on him, pinning him underneath and crushing him to death. I'm so sorry." I went into shock! It was totally unexpected. The next few days were a blur.

You need to understand some of the implications to my becoming a widow. In my world my status immediately changed into that of a second-class citizen. It was as though I became invisible. He had no pension to leave us; we had no health insurance or life insurance like you have. He only left us our humble little house and small plot of ground. Now it was totally, and I mean totally, up to me to feed and sustain my son and myself.

To complicate things, our area began experiencing a famine—no water, no rain, and so no crops. My garden withered, my olive tree died, the fig tree stopped bearing fruit, and our two goats had to be sold because there was no food for them. Rather quickly, I became a pauper. Bare existence was all I could manage. Prices of food took a big jump, and my money was soon gone. We were slowly starving. I could barely stand to look into the sunken eyes of my son.

Then, this day arrived. There was just enough flour and a little bit of oil in a jug to make our last meal that would consist of a few bites between us. We just needed two sticks to burn to bake the bread. I had planned this last day with my son. We'd eat, go to bed at dusk and lay in bed until we died. I had no other choices.

While I was scrounging for the two sticks, my attention was drawn to this man coming towards me. He looked like he was very hungry, too. At first, because of his appearance, I was afraid of him. No one else was around, and I couldn't even run from him. He had long straggly hair and a beard that flowed to his chest. He was dressed in some kind of animal skins and was quite a sight.

As he approached, he smiled, the first time anybody had smiled at me since my husband had died. He seemed kindly enough.

In a gentle voice, he asked, "Would you please get me a cup of water?"

"Sure, just wait here," I replied as I turned back to the house. I had gone only a few short steps when he called out after me.

"Please, bring me some bread, too."

Was this a mad man or something? I thought. *He could just as well ask me for the moon.* This was really hard for me because my parents (who were also dead and gone) taught me to help strangers when possible. *But this is a grown man, strong and healthy, and he asks me, a starving widow, to give him something to eat. What's the matter with him?*

I turned and faced him. I wasn't too happy about helping this guy. I said, and not too kindly, either, "Listen, here's my story. As surely as your God lives, I don't have any bread! I have a handful of flour and a dab of oil in my jug, just enough for my son and me. I was just going to make it, and after we ate, we were going to lay down and die."

He smiled back and made his request again, "Go home and bake your bread but make me a loaf first."

Of all the nerve! He wanted it first! Didn't he see how emaciated I was, and how much I was in need of this bread? Then it dawned on me that he was probably some kind of preacher. It was just like those preachers, always making demands on poor people, putting themselves first. He made me mad.

He smiled at me and continued, "The Lord God of Israel says, if you do so, the jar of flour will not be used up and the jug of oil will not run dry until the famine is over!"

I was astounded! I blurted out, "Who are you, anyway?"

"Elijah, the prophet—the man who confronted the king and told him there would be no more rain for the next three and half years."

When he said "Elijah," I knew I had heard about him and his exploits. I knew he was a wanted man in Israel. Then I became afraid because to hide him could be dangerous for us. But his promises were almost too good to be true. I decided to go and do as he said.

You'll never believe what happened. I made his loaf of bread first, and while it was baking, I went back to make another loaf. There was still just as much flour in the bowl as before, and the oil in the jug was at the same level. I pulled the one cake out of the oven for Elijah and mixed up another one for me, and the flour level was the same, and the oil was the same! This went on for weeks, months and then into years. Sure enough, every time I needed to bake, flour and oil were always there!

Since the man needed a place to hide, I offered our upstairs room to him. He stayed out of sight. If an errand needed to be run, I did it for him. I cooked his meals and cleaned his room. He was a delightful man. The stories he told were fascinating. He shared with us all about his God and how powerful He is. During those years, we ate miracles every day! As long as Elijah stayed with us, I knew we'd be safe and well fed.

Then more tragedy happened. My son got sick and in a couple of days died while I was holding him. I was grieving but angry.

I confronted Elijah, "Why did you come to my house—to remind me of my sin and kill my son?"

He simply said, "Give me your son." I reluctantly gave him my dead son and Elijah carried him upstairs. I couldn't help but overhear him praying, "O Lord my God, why have you done this? She is helping me and now this!" There was quiet, then I heard him pray three times, louder each time, "Lord, let this boy live! Let this boy's life return! God, let him come back to life!" All was quiet, and then I heard him on the steps.

Elijah came down, holding my living son, and both of them were grinning ear to ear. I hugged Elijah and held my son close. He was dead but now was alive. What a God! What a prophet! This miracle was another confirmation to me that Elijah was a man of God. I held my son, and over and over I exclaimed, "It's a miracle! It's a miracle!"

Elijah encouraged me to give God praise and thanks. My

heart was so full, I couldn't find words, other than to say, "Thank You, Lord! Thank You, Lord."

Every day we experienced a miracle, so when Elijah asked me to give him my dead son, I just believed in him and trusted. I didn't know what was going to happen. But it was a miracle! I wanted to shout it from the housetops, but didn't because I wanted to hide Elijah as long as he needed us. For hours on end, he and my son played together. It was so great having a man around the house.

In the third year, one morning over breakfast I knew something was up. Elijah gently explained to us that it was time for him to leave us and confront the king of Israel. He profusely thanked me for my kindness and told me not to worry because he knew the rains would come back in a few days. He promised the flour and oil would last until we had a crop in our garden, which proved to be true. He gave me a big hug, picked up my son, held him, and told him to be a good boy and take care of his mother because he would be the man of the house now. He gave him a kiss and fondly patted him on the head and left. Just like that he was gone. I was so sorry he had to leave.

Now I was free to share the wonder of my miracle. Neighbors had wondered how we had managed to survive. Now I could tell them my story. I invited them in to see how it worked—I took out flour and there was still the same amount left. I poured out the oil and still the same amount was present in the bottom of the jug. It still amazed me and confounded all of them. It caused some major excitement in our neighborhood, so I demonstrated it over and over. And I told them about my son dying and coming back to life. That really caused a sensation. People wanted to know about this miracle-working God of Israel and Elijah. I had often pondered on why it had been that a poor widow, such as me, would hide the prophet in a foreign land for three and half years. Why didn't God hide him with a widow in Israel?

We never saw Elijah again. Things turned around for us. My son grew up to be a fine young man who took care of me in my old age. He became a businessman and quite wealthy, and I know it was because of God's blessing.

I had not heard the unbelievable news about Elijah and his calling fire down from heaven on the top of Mt. Carmel until he left. I believed it for fact. With a God like his, I knew anything was possible!

WISDOM FROM A WIDOW FOR 21st CENTURY LIVING:

God does not and will not ignore the needs in your life. In this case, He didn't give too much nor too little, but just enough. It was a day-at-a-time kind of miracle. It became a daily walk of faith. King David noticed this kind of provision when he said, "I was young, but now I'm old. But I have never seen the righteous forsaken nor their seed begging for bread."

There's one more nugget we see here and that is to obey God. Be willing to entertain strangers because you might entertain an angel or a prophet of God and not even know it. God is still the miracle provider—even today and in your situation!

Chapter Nineteen

QUEEN ESTHER

Desperate to save her people

 We know little of this lady and her background. We do know she was born into a family that had been captured and taken to the Persian Empire's capital city of Susa (or Shushan). Later, the Jews were allowed to return to Jerusalem, but Esther's family decided to stay in Persia along with thousands more. This story took place about 600 B.C.

Hadassah was her given name. Her parents died when she was a young child, and she came under the care of Mordecai, who was a palace official. There is some controversy regarding this relationship—some say he was a cousin, others say he was an uncle. Whatever he was, he raised her as his own daughter. And she loved and obeyed him even after she became queen.

Scripture: *The Book of Esther (It's best if you can read it in a single sitting.)*

HER SIDE OF THE STORY...

I was born into a Jewish family and was an only child. We lived in the royal city of Shushan, the capital of the Persian Empire. They named me Hadassah. We really were slaves, and both Mom and Dad toiled for the Empire. Our nation, Israel, had been defeated years ago, and we had been taken here. Many of our people returned to Jerusalem some years ago, but Mom and Dad decided to remain here in Shushan. We really had it pretty good.

But when I was still a little girl, both my parents died. I would have been left alone, but thankfully, my Uncle Mordecai took me in and raised me as if I was his own daughter. He was wonderful and I loved him dearly. He had worked his way up to being part of the official palace administration. He was smart, and the Persians promoted him.

You might not believe what happened next—Queen Vashti refused to obey one of King Xerxes' direct commands! The media carried the story. It was all we heard for days. Everyone was talking about it. This was sensational! One of the seven princes of the kingdom demanded she be killed before all the wives in the empire did the same to their husbands. It was sort of laughable, but no one dared laugh out loud!

The women were saying to each other, "Go girl! Good for you!" The men were afraid they might have a rebellion on their hands and shouted, "Something must be done about this woman and all other women like her!" It was the hottest issue in our day.

All the king's advisors were incensed, "If your wife refused His Majesty's order, soon all wives will refuse their husbands! This can't be allowed to stand! Punish her!" The account says the king "banished" her so that she would never appear before him again.

King Xerxes became lonely and needed a new queen, so his advisors devised a beauty contest to be held in all the provinces to find the most beautiful girl. Mordecai entered my name and I was chosen to be sent to the king's harem. Each of us was assigned seven helpers to make us beautiful and were enrolled in a one-year program to prepare us. We all wanted to be crowned queen, and the other girls vied with one another, picturing how they could enjoy all the servants, money, prestige, fame, and power that came with the crown! I didn't want or need all this stuff; I was just little ol' me, a Jewish slave girl, really a P.O.W. and ethnic to boot. My turn came to go to the king and I asked for nothing except what the King's eunuch—one smart cookie—advised me to take. And I won the crown hands down! Imagine, I won the prize and the king's heart! I was humbled; I advanced from being a slave girl to a queen of the most powerful empire in the world.

I could end my story right here because it's a great ending, but there's more to it. After I became the queen, Mordecai uncovered a conspiracy to kill the king and got word to me, and I warned the king. They caught the guys and hanged them. This became part of the royal diary.

Next came the scary part. Uncle Mordecai, bless his heart, lit the fuse that set off the fireworks that followed. There was this pompous guy, Haman, top advisor to the king who loved to lord it over everybody else. He made sure everybody knew who he was and how they must all bow to the ground in his presence. Talk about an ego trip! And because of his power and control, everybody did bow before him except Uncle Mordecai. Mordecai flat told him he didn't bow to any man, but he bowed to God. Haman, to say the least, was really ticked. Oh, how he hated my kind and gentle uncle.

In order to get at Mordecai and force him to bow to him, he devised a diabolical plan to ethnically cleanse all the Jews from the kingdom. This plan was sent to all the provinces, and the city was in a turmoil. Mordecai caught wind of it and related the scheme to me. My uncle made sure I understood that my life and the life of all the Jews in the country were on the line.

Mordecai said the only way I could save myself and the

necks of all the Jews was to approach the king and plead for our lives. That was a whole lot easier said than done. Anyone who entered the royal throne room without being invited would quickly lose his life unless the king held out his golden scepter. It was scary. My uncle wanted me to go uninvited to the king and plead our cause.

I called for a three-day period of fasting and prayer by our people and prepared myself in the king's favorite outfit, put on my best smile, and humbly entered and stood by the door. I knew I was taking my life in my hands—but when he saw me, he liked what he saw and held out his golden scepter. He came down from the throne and hugged me, looked into my eyes and said, "Beautiful, I love you. I love you so much I'd give you half of my kingdom." I knew, or at least I hoped, this was going to work out.

I really kind of lost my tongue. The suspense, the possible brush with death almost did me in. Finally, I managed, "How about if you and Haman come to my quarters for a special meal?" There's nothing like filling a man's stomach with a feast to put him in a good mood.

It was a festive meal with the king, Haman, and me. The king finally asked, "My love, what is it you want?"

I lost my nerve when the wicked Haman looked at me. I squeaked out, "Let's do this again tomorrow night." It was agreed. They left in high spirits, and I breathed a sigh of relief and wondered why I had lost my nerve and not told him the real story. The next night I knew I would.

Haman was whistling a happy tune and walked out the palace gate and bumped into Mordecai. You guessed it! People had bowed and scraped all the way out, but not good old Uncle Mordy. He just smiled a sly little smile and stood ramrod stiff. There would be no bowing from him.

Haman pouted and plotted all the way home! His wife

said, "Build a 75-foot gallows and ask the king to let you hang the old man on it!" Grabbing her idea, he hired some laborers right away and had it built all through the night.

It must have been the hammering that kept the king awake that night. He tried it all—hot milk, buttered toast, pills from the doctor, counting sheep. Nothing helped; it was just a sleepless night. Finally he commanded that the official diary be brought to him so he could read himself to sleep. Fortunately, he read about the time my uncle had uncovered the plot to have him killed.

He sat bolt upright in bed and shouted to his sleepy attendant, "Did we ever honor Mordecai for this good deed?"

"No," the attendant replied. "Why don't you try and go to sleep again?"

In the morning, the king grabbed Haman who happened to be close by and asked, "Haman, what should I do to a man whom the king wants to honor?"

Haman thought, *Who could the king possibly have in mind, except me? Let's make this good. What an opportunity to build up my image!* Poor guy, he didn't see it coming.

He cleared his throat, threw his shoulders back and laid it all out, "Let him wear the king's royal purple robe, ride in the king's chariot, and wear the king's crown. Have somebody walk in front of him proclaiming in a loud voice, 'This is how the king gives honor to a very special man!' I think that should do."

I wasn't there, but I was told the next moment was absolutely priceless. Haman waited for the king's reply, but when he received it, it punctured his balloon.

"Good thinking, Haman, now do everything you have said for Mordecai!" What a parade it was! Uncle Mordecai enjoyed every minute with Haman out in front shouting, "This is the king's man, a man the king honors!" It was a spectacle to end all spectacles. The people who knew the inside scoop were in stitches.

125

Haman finally arrived home, exhausted, beat, embarrassed, angry, frustrated, and royally humiliated. He didn't have time to change when the king's eunuchs took him to my second banquet. I took one look at Haman and read the kind of day he'd had. I almost lost it. The meal was wonderful; the king was in a great mood.

Then the king asked again, "Darling, this has been a most wonderful evening. Now ask me anything, and I'll do it for you."

Bravely, I told him about the vile decree to kill all the Jews in the land, including me.

Incensed, he asked, "Who is the turkey responsible for this?"

And I was ready! I pointed at the cowering Haman and shouted, "The enemy is this vile, despicable Haman!"

There's anger and then there's a king's anger! Nobody gets mad like a king. Kings can do things with their anger, and that's why a king is such a dangerous enemy if aroused. He jumped to his feet and looked out the window, then stepped out into the palace garden. I know he was thinking about how to handle this.

Haman stayed behind to grovel and beg for his life. Just when the king returned to the banquet room, Haman threw himself over me on my reclining couch—a real "No, no"! The king's anger went to another level and he shouted, "Will this turkey even molest my queen in my house?"

The palace bodyguards came running, threw Haman to the floor, tied him up, and put a hood over his face. He was screaming and crying as they dragged him out. Harbona, one of the king's eunuchs, jumped in and said, "I know what to do with him. He made a 75-foot gallows in his front yard intended for Mordecai—why not hang him high!"

The king loved it, and said, "Hang him!" It took a bit, but

the king's fury cooled. He sat down on my couch, lovingly took me into his arms and said, "My dearest wife, what a close call. I could have lost you, too, to this madman and his schemes."

I was told the hanging was quite a spectacle. The guards dragged a screaming and protesting Haman down the street. Torches were lit, the commotion roused people, and soon there was a huge crowd following them.

The guards shouted, "We are hanging this man on the king's orders."

You need to understand—a good hanging was a great free show. People loved it. They shouted and hollered and joined in the fun. There, for all the world to see, on his 75-foot gallows, Haman was unceremoniously hanged. It was quite a shock to his wife, his family and his friends. That's not all, the king gave me all his holdings as a reward. In turn, I gave these to Mordecai for his retirement.

One more thing needed to be done; it was now a simple matter. The king needed another decree to counter the one he had authorized. He couldn't take back the original order to kill all the Jews, but he allowed Mordecai and me to write a new law authorizing all the Jews on the specified days to arm themselves and kill anybody who attempted to kill them. Some of the Jews used this as an excuse to right some wrongs and killed more than a thousand of their enemies. It was quite a day!

The next year and every year following, my people turned this commemoration into a festival. Jews all over the world celebrated the first day of "Purim" with worship and fasting, and the second day is given to rejoicing, food, dancing, special music, dramas and more.

I must tell you, as a result of all this, Mordecai was promoted to be the number two man under the king. Imagine, a Jew was now number two in the Persian Empire. It was like

Joseph, another Jew who went from being a slave to the number two guy in Egypt. God sure has a great sense of humor.

What about me? After all this excitement settled down, I lived out my life as the Queen of Persia—the most powerful woman in the land even though I was once a humble Jewish slave. What's important is not what Mordecai or I have done, but as I look back over my life, I see what God has done in it all. God knew long before all these events He needed to place somebody in the right place for the right time to spare His people. It just so happened that person was me.

WISDOM FROM QUEEN ESTHER FOR 21st CENTURY LIVING:

There is so much to glean from this story. Let's start with the awesomeness of a God who uses the most unlikely of people to fulfill His purposes. He promotes a Jewish orphan, a nobody who becomes a somebody, who is willing to risk her life to make a positive commitment in order to help others.

Maybe this is enough. You can draw other lessons for yourself. But I must ask you if you are willing to allow God to use you to accomplish His purposes in your world. Perhaps all of us have hidden behind excuses that we have no talents and no influence, and that we are full of imperfections. God isn't especially looking for talented people or perfect people—God is looking for willing people! All your previous life experiences have prepared you for the challenges you face today.

Chapter Twenty

GOMER

Desperate to feel loved

Gomer is the woman made infamous for her prostitution and marriage to one of God's prophets, Hosea. Her story is a living allegory, a life lesson for the nation in which she and her husband lived. She was an example of what was happening in her nation. Her name means "completion" or more literally, the "filling up of the measure of idolatry" or "full of wickedness."

She was the daughter of Diblaim whose name signifies "double layers of grape-cake." It's a picture of a man given over to a debauched lifestyle. With such a father as an example, Gomer became a woman in pursuit of a sensual life. Then she married Hosea, the godly prophet and became a symbol of God's grace. It's a fascinating story of God's love.

Scripture: *Hosea 1:1-11; 3:1-5 (This entire book is a love story of how a loving God goes in search for his wayward, people.)*

HER SIDE OF THE STORY...

Morning finally began to dawn. I was cold, shivering from the night cold. I reached for a meager blanket, but I found no warmth there. The first rays of the sun began penetrating the darkness of my cell. This was the longest night of my wretched life. The sun brought no relief. I sat up and stretched. I had spent the night on this cold stone floor. I managed to get to my feet, and my ankle chain rattled on the stones. I shuddered. I dreaded this day like no other. I was going to be sold on the auction block just like a common slave! I pictured the auctioneers chanting, "My friends, look what we have here! The prophet's wife is to be sold! Who'll start the bidding?" Involuntarily, a moan escaped my lips. I wrapped my arms around my wasted body—imagine, me a slave! I'm as low in the gutter as you can get.

I guess I'm a bit ahead of myself. Do you mind if I bring you up to speed? My childhood was rotten and helped start me down the path I eventually took as an adult.

As soon as I could, I ran away from home and became one of those infamous homeless types you read so much about. I did the only thing I could figure out—I sold my body to the highest bidder and became a prostitute. I made good money and soon was able to have my own apartment. I was young and a looker. I took good care of myself because to let myself go would have been bad for business.

I know all you good people don't understand my world, but I was honest and developed a good clientele. Really, underneath my façade, I was a good person with a good heart.

In my business you hear all the gossip out on the street. Word kept coming to me about this prophet guy, Hosea. He was powerful and purportedly one handsome hunk. I wanted to meet him.

I made sure it happened. I was soliciting business on a particular street corner when I spotted him coming in my direction. He was tall, a commanding presence with the kindest look on his face. Something immediately drew me to him.

Now, I'm a pretty good judge of men with all my experience, but this guy, there was something different about him. He had an aura I couldn't explain.

He was looking right at me, up and down. He got real close and fastened his dark brown eyes on me. His opening line, "Would you be so kind as to allow me to buy you a cup of tea?"

I didn't know how to reply; no man had ever made this kind of an invitation. I managed to blurt out, "Okay...sure." He took me by the arm and steered me to the nearest shop.

He ordered the teas and brought two sweet delicacies. The conversation never got around to my occupation. For the first time in my life I had butterflies in my stomach. It was weird. As quickly as it began, our time together ended; he had an appointment to keep and asked if we could meet again.

Sure enough, every day for the next week, I had tea with this guy. You should have heard the gossips crowing. "Gomer, the prostitute, is having tea with our local preacher!" It was kind of cute. I enjoyed it; it lifted my image from the gutter to the next level anyway. Besides, he was good company. He stretched my mind and challenged me in many ways.

How long would this go on? I didn't know. Not once did he flirt with me or come on to me. This was most unusual; it'd never happened to me before. Honestly, I think I was falling in love for the first time in my life. Most of the guys I had known were nothing more than a payday; no emotion was involved, just animal lust in action. Now I was caught by this wonderful man.

I was dumfounded when Hosea proposed marriage! I could hardly imagine his wanting to be married to me, a prostitute. He knew who I was and where I had come from. He laid down only one stipulation—I was not to take another lover. I was to be his wife and his wife only. He asked if I could do it.

"Yes, I could live with you and have a monogamous relationship." I promised him and really meant it.

To say the least, our wedding caused a sensation. The temple was packed with curiosity seekers. I had never been treated like a lady by any man, ever in my life. This was like heaven to me.

I could never quite figure out why Hosea had married me. I certainly was no virgin. I gradually began to see that we were characters in a little play written and produced by his God. Our marriage had made front page news all across Israel. We were the most famous couple in the land.

It soon began to dawn me—I was a pawn, again! This time God was using me, using us. I began to resent it. The picture began to come clearer in my mind; Hosea was cast as the "God" figure, the good loving husband. I was featured as the unfaithful wife, like the nation of Israel had become unfaithful to God, its lover.

It came to a head in my mind when our first son was born. We couldn't even name our children. This God told my husband to name our first "Jezreel." Who in their right mind would give a kid a name meaning "the valley of both crime and punishment"? He and the rest of our kids became characters in this morality play of this all powerful God.

I found myself resenting, not Hosea so much, but this God he supposedly was serving. I didn't mean to, but I met one of my former best-paying customers on the street. When he propositioned me, reluctantly I caved in and serviced him. It was good money.

Our second child was born, and this naming bit was worse. She was to be named "Lo-ruhamah." Can you imagine what this did to an innocent child? Who would name a little girl "not loved!" Unbelievable! My anger increased—why should one little girl have to carry all the punishment for an entire nation? My resentment grew. I really looked with longing on my past life. The opportunities were there, and I began to take them.

Hosea was wonderful beyond words. He continually reassured me of his undying love, and I trampled on it by shouting at him, "You knew what I was when you married me. What did you expect?"

You could say I was the one who faithfully carried out the role into which God had cast me. I thought it funny—He knew I could play it to the hilt and so I did. Without me, there would not have been a story.

Our third child was born, and I was almost positively sure that Hosea was not the father and he knew it, too. But this wonderful God had a name already picked out, "Lo-ammi." And this was the final straw that broke the camel's back. I couldn't believe it! Why saddle a kid with a horrid name he would have to deal with for his entire life—"you are not my people!" This poor kid went through life thinking he didn't belong because he was disowned from birth. Oh, Hosea was a good daddy, and I was a good mommy when I wasn't bombed out with my booze or drugs.

As soon as he was weaned, I left home. I walked out on my three, poor little babies and loving husband. Our last night together at the supper table still haunts me. I had already made my plans—it was back on the streets with no more of this God stuff for me. I'd take the love, such as it was, from admirers who wanted my body for a night. Hosea fed the kids, bathed them, tucked them into bed, said their prayers and kissed them goodnight. I was lost in my own little world. Finally, I roused myself enough to creep in and kiss them good-bye through my tears. It was a heart-wrenching experience. I knew I would miss them, but you do what you have to do. The worst part was leaving the love of Hosea. But he knew something was up.

He held me close for the longest time and said it again, "Honey, I love you! No matter what you have done or will do in the future, know that I will always love you."

He finally dropped off to sleep. Carefully, so as to not disturb him, I picked up my bag and let myself out into the night. My current lover was waiting for me in his chariot down the block and around the corner. He gave me a big kiss and off we went.

Business wasn't so good this go-round. Well, what did you expect? Me? An aging prostitute with wrinkles and after three kids, stretch marks everywhere. I noticed lots of my first timers never came back. I was almost reduced to begging for another job. I lowered my prices and hit the bottle more often. In a matter of months, the truth really hit me. Why had I left my prophet husband and my three kids for this? But I was too proud to go back home. Life just got worse and worse. I couldn't pay my rent, and soon I was homeless. My self-esteem was shot. I was a miserable nothing.

I sold myself as a slave to a horrid, mean-tempered slob of a man. He had money but that's all. He laughed at me, degraded me and ridiculed me until he tired of his little games and put me up for sale in the slave auction. He said, "Maybe you will bring a few bucks. If I am lucky, maybe enough to buy another donkey."

My breakfast was a crust of bread and half a glass of water. The auctioneer came by with some of his help and gave them directions. "See what you can do to clean her up. Make her over." And so I was subjected to all kinds of indignities as they attempted a hair make-over, a bath to get rid of the lice, lots of make-up to cover the lines, and a sexy dress to show the merchandise. I could not have been more humiliated!

The auction went on, and I could hear the banter between the auctioneer and buyers. "Sold!" Each time I shivered when I heard the gavel bang.

I was the last slave on the auction block. Finally, they came for me. "Head up and shoulders back," they told me. "Walk as if you were alive. Girl, this is your lucky day. You will be sold to the highest bidder, hahaha!"

When I was paraded out into the light, I blinked. I was lifted up to the auction block and told to walk back and forth and twirl around so all could see the merchandise. There is no humiliation equal to these moments.

The auctioneer banged his gavel for silence. "Gomer is the prophet's wife. How would you like to take the wife of a holy man to your home?" More laughter! The sarcasm could be cut with a knife. The auctioneer enjoyed this; the crowd loved it. I was the whipping girl. They laid it on.

"Who will start the bidding?"

I was insulted—the bidding began with a single half-shekel—only about 38 cents! Was that all I was worth? I couldn't help myself; I began to silently cry, tears trickling down both cheeks. My make-up began to run. The crowd enjoyed the show and laughed all the more. The bidding gradually went up. I was pathetic, standing with head bowed as the humiliation was heaped on me. There was no place to hide.

The bidding grew more frenzied until I heard an unmistakable voice. Could it be? This voice kept raising the bid. Yes! It was unbelievable. I began to hope. There it was again and again. It was Hosea! How did he get here? Why was he bidding? Did he still love me? My heart began racing. Would he win out?

He made the final bid, "fifteen shekels of silver and a homer and a half of barley!" I held my breath! He'd shouted it out so all could hear in that powerful preacher voice of his. Nobody else raised the bid.

I heard, "Going once, going twice, and gone! To Hosea the preacher, who is out of his mind to buy back a wretched wife such as this." They all hooted and laughed again.

But he caught my eye as he muscled his way through the crowd. When he stopped to settle up with the cashier, he looked at me with the look of love. I melted, and the tears really flowed. He took his bill of sale and came up on the auction block, wrapped me in one of my shawls, held me tight, reached up one hand to wipe away my tears, and kissed me in full sight of the crowd. They were stunned into silence. He picked me up and carried me off that horrid auction block and took me to his waiting camel.

He helped me up onto the back saddle, and we were off. I was speechless. I didn't know what to say. I just sat there, holding onto him, not knowing whether to shout or cry, smile or weep. I was totally embarrassed. I was overcome with emotion. This was more than I ever dreamed.

He turned to me, not with condemnation but with love, and spoke first, "Darling, you are going to spend all the rest of your life with me. We'll grow old together. I only ask one thing: Don't go looking for love in any other place. I love you and will always love you with all my heart."

I was speechless. There were no lectures, no other conditions, no penance, or no repentance asked of me. Just acceptance and love from Hosea.

"Now, dear, I've reserved a little room for us away from here, right next to the Mediterranean. It's a romantic get-a-way for the two of us for the next three days. It'll help you recover before we go home to see the kids. And I packed your bags with your clothes. Okay?"

What could I say? I looked at him and said, "Really? I don't deserve this. I ran away from home…I've dragged your name in the mud…I've…." And he reached over and gently placed his finger on my lips, sealing them. Inside, I couldn't explain what was happening. I was beginning to come alive, to live again, like a resurrection from the dead.

Don't get me wrong, I had to dry out and get myself back on track. But I did. Then it was time to go back home to my little kiddies. I know they had grown while I was gone. Hosea told me all of their milestones. I couldn't wait to hold my babies again!

As we rode up the driveway, there were these three little bodies jumping up and down and yelling, "Momma! Momma! Mommmaaa!" Tears were flowing; never have I been greeted so warmly. What a wonderful five-way family hug we had. I almost burst from the outpouring of love into my empty soul.

I just knew it—we were going to make it this time! And, we did. We lived happily ever after. Under the ministry of Hosea, our land experienced a revival. Never again did I wander or even desire to leave.

As I look back, I made lots of mistakes. I accepted God's forgiveness. I finally came to the place where I wasn't bitter toward God, and I wouldn't ask Him to re-write the script. I was finally able to also forgive myself. Our family story and lifestyle became a living example of the great love God has for a lost people and a lost nation!

WISDOM FROM THE LIFE OF GOMER FOR 21st CENTURY LIVING:

The image of Gomer, to many people, is one of the most distasteful stories of the Bible. Some have attempted to explain it away as being nothing but an allegory, a story, an illustration. But Gomer is specifically named as are her children. No, the story is true and should be here because of one fabulous truth: GOD LOVES YOU AND ME, NO MATTER HOW FAR WE MIGHT HAVE FALLEN, AND OFFERS US FORGIVENESS AND MERCY!

My friend, are you willingly walking away from God and His love? Are you rebelling against His love? Would you rather do your own thing? Know that at some time in your life, you will hit bottom. Then where will you turn for help? Will it take hitting bottom before you are willing to accept His forgiveness, His mercy, His grace, His love? Don't wait that long! He is a God of love and mercy and freely makes it available to you and me. We might not understand how He can do such a thing, but we should always remember the story of Gomer and Hosea and God's love!

Chapter Twenty-One

REBEKAH

Desperate to see her son succeed

This story is one of romance and a happy home until the twins arrived. The story in Genesis 24 is one of the most sublime and beautiful stories in all of romantic literature. It has all the elements for a happy read.

Rebekah's name is filled with romantic visions. Its root can be found in a noun meaning the "hitching place." Now don't jump to your conclusion just yet. It was connected with a "tied-up calf or lamb," particularly one that is choice and plump. When applied to a girl, the concept is that she has a beauty by which men are snared, lassoed or captured. A broader meaning is that she was a "captivating" female. And the noose was firmly looped around the neck of Isaac. Today in many parts of the world, Rebekah or Rebecca is a name many mothers use for their little girls.

Scripture: *Genesis 22:23-24; 24:1-67; 25:20-28; 26:6-28:9; 29:12; 35:8; 49:31; Romans 9:6-16*

HER SIDE OF THE STORY...

It was an ordinary day in our hauntingly beautiful desert. My favorite time of the day is when the sun is dipping just beyond the western rim of the sky painting everything a golden hue. I loved it. I was on my way to do my regular chores, fetching water from the well just outside our little town of Nahor located about 500 miles northeast of Canaan. Many other women had also come. This was where the gossips got all the grist for their mill. It was fun and I always picked up the latest and juiciest tidbits.

At first I didn't notice, but there was a stranger with ten kneeling, thirsty camels. They had obviously come a long way. The lone stranger seemed to be deep in thought and obviously looking for something. I was curious—was he looking at me? He sauntered closer and politely asked for a drink of cool water, and I gave it to him.

Then I looked at his camels, which were obviously thirsty. I loved animals and immediately detected they needed water. I offered, "I bet your camels are plenty thirsty. I'll water them, too." Do you have any idea how much water thirsty camels can drink? I thought my arms would fall off before they were satisfied. I glanced at this stranger between buckets of water. I discovered that all the while he was giving me a strange look, as if he were sizing me up. Mostly, he studied my face. Each time I glanced in his direction he was looking; it made me feel a bit strange. It wasn't a sinister look or even a sensual look. It was a studious, wondering, curious look. Each time I caught his eye, I gave him a smile.

The camels finally had enough. I was beat and sat down on a nearby bench. He came over to me and introduced himself, "I'm Eliezer, number one servant of my master Abraham."

I replied, "My name is Rebekah. My father's name is Bethuel, and my grandfather's name is Abraham." Eliezer just about jumped out of his skin!

Quickly he replied, "I am here looking for a bride for Abraham's son, Isaac! And honey, I think you're the one. I'm quite sure the hand of God is in this chance meeting!"

I didn't know how to answer this stranger. He reached into a saddle bag and pulled out gorgeous pieces of jewelry—a gold nose ring and two gold bracelets. Never had I seen such jewelry! The rock in the ring was a stunner. I put them on and they fit like they were made for me. I brushed the sweat out of my eyes to be able to see more clearly—they were pure gold.

This man represented money, big money! I invited him home with his ten camels. "Sure, we've got room for you." You should have seen the look on my mother's face when she spotted my jewelry and my huge smile. All this because I had watered camels! My brother, Laban, and Dad carefully eyed the camels and this Eliezer guy. It didn't take them long to determine this was an important man who must represent a really important man. The whole caravan, pure-bred camels, the saddles, the harnesses, and his clothes all reeked of m-o-n-e-y! I was just jumping inside with excitement. What does all this mean?

Soon Eliezer and my dad were deep into a Middle-Eastern type of bargaining. This guy was so excited because he believed it was God who had set up our meeting, and he was positive I was the dream girl for Isaac!

Early the next morning, over breakfast, the deal had been done and now he wanted to take me immediately and set out for his home. He said something about the fact that Abraham was so old he might kick the bucket at any moment, which forced him to hurry!

My brother Laban and Mom said, "This is too quick. Give us ten days and then she can go."

Eliezer replied, "No way. Rebekah is the one! Don't delay me. My Master is waiting!"

My father, mother, brothers and sisters all turned in my direction. Daddy said, "Honey, you decide. Will you go with this man?" Finally, for the first time, they asked me. It was all about me in the first place. You know, it took me about two seconds to answer.

"Yes, I will go with him!" I know it was a spur of the moment decision, but my heart jumped inside and told me it was the right thing to do! I quickly packed a travel bag. Eliezer told me not to worry about clothes, to take just enough to get me home to Canaan.

I really think Laban and my daddy were a little bit disappointed. They had been eyeing all the goods packed in the saddle bags and had been scheming how to get some of this booty. But as soon as Eliezer heard my answer, he gave me more gold and silver jewelry and a complete new wardrobe! He then heaped up some of the most exotic gifts for Mom and Dad and my brother and sisters. It was like Christmas morning in your day.

My family blessed me, and we were on our way. My nurse came with me, and she was excited about a new adventure, too! It took us about two weeks; my suspense was almost unbearable.

I peppered Eliezer with questions. I asked him to tell me all about my new husband. Was he tall? Was he good looking? I didn't have to ask if he was rich because he already told me he would inherit all of Abraham's holdings, who happened to be the richest man in the world, well almost, anyway. Was Isaac kind and gentle? Would he be pleased with me? How old was he? I pumped him until he got tired of me asking. It was all so romantic and exciting—every girl's dream.

On the fourteenth day, I looked out across the desert hills. It was about dusk, my favorite time, and I spotted this guy looking for something, coming in my direction. I asked Eliezer, "Is it him?"

"Yes."

"Stop this camel!" I shouted. "I've got to change my

clothes, put on some make up, wipe off the dust; quick, somebody help me!" I jumped off the camel and did a quick change. I put on my best veil and best dress along with my best smile.

Eliezer went on ahead, and I overheard him tell Isaac all the exciting news. As Eliezer talked, Isaac kept looking in my direction. I can't describe the moment, but my butterflies were hatching more butterflies! Would he really like what he was about to see? Would he love me? I believed I was already deeply in love with him, or at least the description Eliezer had painted of him. What if he sent me back home? Oh, Lord, my knees are shaking; he's coming toward me. Oh, what should I say? How should I act? He's forty years old, twice my age! Dear God, what have I gotten myself into? He stopped in front of me and looked deeply into my eyes. He looked stunned, too, and smiled.

He came closer, "Mind if I take your hand?" I couldn't speak, I just nodded. He took both of mine in his and held me. Shivers went from the tips of my fingers up my arms and down my spine!

"May I lift your veil?" Again I nodded.

He reached and lifted it up; I searched his eyes. They opened in surprise; he really smiled wide this time. He liked what he was seeing, and I liked what I was experiencing. He gently placed an arm about my waist and led me to his home. He didn't say much, but I heard him whistle a happy tune.

We had a simple wedding—just family, Eliezer and family servants. It was candlelight, wine and roses. Romantic! He had planned well; then we went to the honeymoon tent. We were madly in love. He told me I had become the comfort of his life, the joy of his life. The only missing ingredient was that his mother didn't have the privilege of meeting me.

Abraham didn't die for a while. In fact, at 140, he was in

fabulous shape, and he took another wife, Keturah. We were both about the same age and had a blast together, just like sisters. She gave Abraham six sons, but Isaac and I were infertile for a long time. Then Abraham died, and we buried him next to Sarah. I must say, it was unbelievable the ways in which God blessed Isaac and, of course, me, too. Our only sorrow was the fact that we had no children.

When Isaac began to pray for a child, I became pregnant after twenty years of waiting! I wasn't as old as Sarah when she gave birth to Isaac, but I felt like it at times. My pregnancy was difficult. Soon it was apparent I was carrying twins—there was a lot of jostling and fighting in my womb.

Then something happened I shall never forget. God spoke to me in an audible voice: "You have two nations in your womb. One son will be stronger than the other. They will war against each other, but the older will serve the younger." I was shocked, and I never told Isaac. This was to be a secret between the Lord and me.

Sure enough, they were born minutes apart with the younger one's little hand grabbing his twin brother's heel and hanging on for dear life. It was cute. We named him "Jacob" the heel-clutcher or heel-grabber. It was not a very nice name, but it suited us. We named the older "Esau," the wild man, and it sure fit him, too. He was born covered with hair. These two grew up, and there was constant competition between them. They fought until it drove Isaac and me nuts.

Esau became a hunter, a rugged outdoors type, handsome, a ladies man, at times violent tempered, impetuous, and a real handful. It was obvious that he loved his dad more than he loved me. Jacob, on the other hand, was given to being thoughtful, introspective, and interested in business matters; he had visions about his future and was strong in different ways. He was determined and he loved me, although he was not a real mommy's boy. We enjoyed long talks, and he was great company for me.

It was kind of sad. I was in my sixties, and no longer the ravaging beauty when Isaac fell in love with me. He was past the hundred mark and showing his age. We didn't have much left in our marriage. Everything centered on our two boys—Isaac loved Esau, and I loved Jacob. That says it all. It's not healthy, but that's the way life had turned for us. It was kind of sad to be divided like this. We were two people living separate lives. We could just as well as have been divorced since we had nothing in common anymore.

We all knew Isaac was getting ready to kick the bucket but when? He was blind as a bat, a bit hard of hearing, arthritic in his old joints, and slow moving. He needed help getting up. And one day it really hit him, "I'm not long for this world; it's time I gave the patriarchal blessing to my oldest son."

He didn't bother to consult with me but just went ahead on his own. Fortunately, I overheard him giving directions to Esau, "Son, today is the day. I'm old and about to die. Go hunt down a choice buck and make some of your famous venison stew. Let's have a little feast, and then I'll give you my blessing for my firstborn son. Hurry! I'll be waiting!"

I immediately took Jacob aside and told him what was happening. I said, "Quick, get me two goats, and we'll make venison stew. Your dad will not know the difference since everything tastes the same to him now. We'll make sure you get the firstborn's blessing!"

Jacob turned to go and said, "Mom, I already stole it from Esau! I never told you, but some time ago, he came in from a hunting trip famished and took one smell of my world famous barbecue and sold the blessing to me for the meal!"

I said, "Great, it's already done; only your Dad doesn't know this. I have a plan for you!"

It didn't take us long until we had the stew ready! I covered Jacob's arms and the back of his neck with goatskins to make him hairy like his brother. And Jacob, with my help, stole the blessing. Isaac didn't suspect a thing. He blessed my Jacob with abundance, the earth's riches, and told him that nations would serve him and people would bow down before him. Here's the best part, he said, "Your brother will bow down to you"—just like the Lord had promised me so long ago. Yes! I did a little victory dance. We did it! It was more than even I expected. You have no idea how powerful is the father's blessing on his firstborn son.

Jacob and I hugged, cried, and declared the day a victory! It didn't last long; we heard Esau coming home. We both hid and listened. It really was so sad; Esau was my son, too. His cry of anguish I'll never forget until the day I die. Shortly afterwards, Isaac died.

I was alone in this world, but not really alone, because I'd have my Jacob. I overheard Esau's threat, "As soon as this funeral is over, I will kill my brother Jacob!" And I knew he was capable of carrying out this threat!

I grabbed Jacob and said, "You've got to leave. Your brother will kill you as soon as your dad's funeral is over. Run to my brother Laban's home in Haran. Stay there until the coast is clear, and I'll send for you."

It was a sad, sad farewell. We clung to each other—mother and favorite son. We cried. Finally, Jacob pulled himself away and started out across the field. He looked back often and waved. It was the saddest day of my life to watch my son walk out of my life. I didn't know it then, but this would be the last time I saw him alive.

Life did go on. Esau stayed around for a while, but he and I didn't get along at all. We fought and bickered. Then he brought home one of those Hittite heathen girls—she was loud, uncouth, and boisterous. I didn't see what Esau saw in her. She became the bitter problem in my life, but they had some sweet grandkids. I guess I became the nasty old mother-in-law to her, but I think she deserved it.

And to top it off, Esau married another of those shameless hussies. I'm almost positive he married these gals just to get my goat. Well, he succeeded!

Word filtered back about what wonderful wives Jacob married and what a wonderful family of twelve boys and one girl they had. I missed out on all of that. I grieved for Jacob, but I never saw him again.

I often wondered if I had done him right. I tell you, God had given me that promise, but I never thought He was there to make sure it was fulfilled, so I took things into my own hands. It may not have been the right thing, but I made sure it accomplished what it was meant to.

WISDOM FROM REBEKAH FOR 21st CENTURY LIVING:

Rebekah must have listened intently to the words of Eliezer about how he had prayed for God's help in finding the right spouse for Isaac. When she responded positively, did she have any idea what that meant? I don't think so. Events leading up to her selection were events orchestrated by God. When confronted with the choice, she was more than willing to allow God's plan to be fulfilled in her life. This is indicated by her answer.

But there is a dark side to the lady. Apparently, their marriage, to begin with, was a wonderful and romantic union. However, time and events changed her, and she showed partiality by loving one son above the other. It tragically divided her home. Isaac loved Esau; Rebekah loved Jacob. Not good. This eventually led to her deceit, a thieving scheme, undercutting her husband, and teaching her son how to deceive. Her later years ended sadly. Rebekah unfortunately seemed to have lost her way when she put one son before the other. We must be careful to keep our priorities straight.

Chapter Twenty-Two

THE PROVERBS 31 HOUSEWIFE

There's no desperation here!

These are the sayings of King Lemuel...an oracle taught to him by his mother. Proverbs 31:1-31

 Many women today consider this "perfect" woman to have been a figment of the imagination of King Lemuel's mother. They say that she was dreaming up the perfect wife for her number one son. Of course, perfection is impossible, but the maturity and responsibility we can learn from these passages are possible. Whether the woman pictured here is real or fictional, we don't know, but she is a woman to be praised and the ideal model for women everywhere.

Likely, no man who has lived on this earth has had as much experience with women as King Solomon. In his book of Proverbs, Solomon wrote about all kinds of women. The opening chapters of his works begin with some very positive pictures of women who are paragons of wisdom in sandals. But mostly, the women he wrote about were harlots, loose women, brazen women, crabby women, strange women, wayward

wives, loud women, lazy women, defiant women, and wives
who are irritating like a drip on a rainy day. To be fair and bal-
anced, he painted men poorly, too. He vividly describes some
men as scoundrels, villains, fools, sluggards, dead-beats, lazy,
sex fiends, and real turkeys. He uses these less-than-glowing
descriptions of men and women to help point out some of the
attitudes and ways that displease God.

To end Solomon's book of Proverbs, we have this wonderful portrayal of a godly woman who blesses the world by
her life. In traditional Jewish homes, husbands and children
often memorized and recited the poem that describes her in
Proverbs 31. Much has been written about her and much can
be learned from her.

A wife of noble character who can find?
    she is worth far more than rubies.
Her husband has full confidence in her
    and lacks nothing of value.
She brings him good, not harm,
    all the days of her life.
She selects wool and flax
    and works with eager hands.
She is like the merchant ships,
    bringing her food from afar.
She gets up while it is still dark;
    she provides food for her family
    and portions for her servant girls.
She considers a field and buys it;
    out of her earnings she plants a vineyard.
She sets about her work vigorously;
    her arms are strong for her tasks.
She sees that her trading is profitable,
    and her lamp does not go out at night.

In her hand she holds the distaff
    and grasps the spindle with her fingers.
She opens her arms to the poor
    and extends her hands to the needy.
When it snows, she has no fear for her household;
    for all of them are clothed in scarlet.
She makes coverings for her bed;
    she is clothed in fine linen and purple.
Her husband is respected at the city gate,
    where he takes his seat among the elders of the land.
She makes linen garments and sells them,
    and supplies the merchants with sashes.
She is clothed with strength and dignity;
    she can laugh at the days to come.
She speaks with wisdom,
    and faithful instruction is on her tongue.
She watches over the affairs of her household
    and does not eat the bread of idleness.
Her children arise and call her blessed;
    her husband also, and he praises her.
Many women do noble things,
    but you surpass them all!
Charm is deceptive, and beauty is fleeting;
    but a woman who fears the Lord is to be praised.
Give her the reward she has earned,
    and let her works bring her praise at the city gate!

The book of Proverbs is crammed full of gems of wisdom for living a lifestyle built on the foundation of wisdom. Really there are only two choices left for all of us—women as well as men. We can either love and embrace wisdom or do our own thing and live a life of foolish decisions.

I believe the virtuous woman portrayed in Proverbs 31 is

meant to inspire both sexes. Think of her life; she inspires us to live productively. Look at what can be accomplished through one woman—homes for others, the needy receiving generosity, employees and clients benefitted by good business practices, and jobs being created. She was filled with serenity. In the end she enjoyed honor, prosperity, a position of leadership for her husband, a future vision of greatness, and a happy family through confidence in her God. Talk about real blessings for your family, friends, spouse and associates! Who wouldn't sing the praises of such people?

As you have read this book, it probably has become evident to you that God loves women, even desperate women, and He will go to great lengths to show them mercy and fulfill their fondest dreams. He has designed a special place for them in His great plan for all mankind.

May God's blessings be upon you as you think about what these women experienced and the wisdom that can be received from a loving God. He can meet the needs of everyone and turn our desperation into fulfillment and joy.